D0149380

I NEVER BELIEVED IN GHOSTS UNTIL...

I NEVER BELIEVED IN GHOSTS UNTIL...

100 Real-Life Encounters

Collected by the Editors of USA WEEKEND

BARNES
&NOBLE
BOOKS
NEW YORK

Copyright © 1992 by USA Weekend, Inc.
All rights reserved.

This edition published by Barnes & Noble, Inc.,
by arrangement with Contemporary Books, Inc.

1994 Barnes & Noble Books

ISBN 1-56619-362-1

Printed and bound in the United States of America

M 9 8 7 6 5 4 3 2 1

CONTENTS

TALES FOR A STORMY NIGHT

LOST SOULS

WHERE SPIRITS DWELL

LOVE THAT CANNOT DIE

HAUNTINGS

THE SHADOW OF DEATH

ACKNOWLEDGMENTS

We wish to thank Constance Kurz of USA WEEKEND for overseeing the project, Stacy Prince of Contemporary Books for shepherding *I Never Believed in Ghosts Until* ... through the editing process, Susan Bokern of Gannett New Business for her guidance, Sandy Graham of USA WEEKEND for identifying the best among the five hundred story submissions, and Kate Bond, Richard Vega, and Gayle Carter of USA WEEKEND for their administrative efforts.

And most of all we want to extend our sincere gratitude to those USA WEEKEND readers who were willing to share their sometimes chilling, always fascinating, encounters with "things that go bump in the night."

INTRODUCTION

There's nothing like a good ghost tale, whether you're a believer or not, to send chills racing up the spine. And apparently the readers of USA WEEKEND agree.

Recently we invited the magazine's readers to send us their stories of the supernatural for a special Halloween feature. We were deluged with more than five hundred stories, six of which we published.

But there were so many more unearthly tales among the growing pile that we were delighted when Contemporary Books asked to publish an anthology of the one hundred best stories. Among our favorites are the ghost who leads a farmer to a hidden murder weapon, the spirit in a pink angora sweater who snaps an Instamatic camera, and the prankish "child" apparition who moves a teddy bear around the house.

Most of our story writers described themselves as skeptics and their ghostly encounters as strictly one-shot visitations. "I've never been accused of being a storyteller or someone who suffers from an overactive imagination," a typical letter began. And a truly surprising number of people started off their stories with "I never believed in ghosts until. . . ."

But some writers claim their house hauntings went on for years. "It's just not something you talked about to those outside the family. What would other people think?" explained one woman who wrote. And a couple, who had agreed not to talk about their "resident spirit" in front of their young children, were later startled to discover that their kids had been seeing the ghost all along and had accepted it as "normal."

Within this anthology, you'll find a smorgasbord of spooks. There are restless spirits who refuse to leave their old stomping grounds and helpful ones who protect the writers from impending danger. There are touching stories of love so strong that it transcends the grave and truly frightening tales of evil presences with superhuman force.

As a general rule, we have changed names, places, and other identifying details to protect the privacy of the people who appear in these stories. Aside from those changes, the voices you hear in these pages are of real-life people and the encounters they believed they had with spirits, both benign and malevolent. Are the visitations real? Coincidence? You be the judge.

—The Editors of USA WEEKEND

I NEVER BELIEVED IN GHOSTS UNTIL...

TALES FOR A STORMY NIGHT

THE HAUNTED FORD

JANET L. HERNANDEZ

In 1960 it was almost impossible to find a good used car for less than $500. With a little help from Dad, I found a 1952 Ford Crestline Victoria, a black and white customized hardtop with a working push-button radio—a bargain at $275.

Since I had recently graduated from high school, money was hard to come by, so I borrowed $250 from Mom and Dad. As soon as I started to work, I would begin to pay off the debt in weekly installments.

Any seventeen-year-old will agree that a "new" car had to be spotless, so Dad and I proceeded to wash and wax my purchase. While buffing the door on the passenger side, we noticed three holes that had been plugged with some sort of patch and repainted. These holes looked like bullet holes, but we didn't care—the car ran pretty well and looked great.

While we were riding around the block on one of our first outings in the car, the vehicle's passenger door flew open. We didn't think much of it and took the car to the garage for repair. The mechanic couldn't find anything wrong with it so he didn't charge us.

The following week, my sister and I were riding around when the same thing happened. As soon as we arrived home, I told Dad. He checked the door catch over again but still could find nothing wrong.

3

The third time it happened, we were driving about forty miles per hour, next to a cemetery. Still we didn't give it much thought.

The fourth time the door flew open, we were also going about forty, this time next to a different cemetery. It was now becoming clear that something strange was going on.

We decided to have the oil changed, so we took the car to our local garage. While the car was up on the lift we noticed that some wires had been fastened to the underside of the car to hold up some of the pipes. This car had been in some sort of mishap. Our bargain was turning into a real mystery! The mechanics secured the wires and added new clamps to the exhaust system. The oil change completed, we went for a spin.

This time we were going fifty miles per hour when the passenger door flew open. Have you ever tried to push a door open at that speed? Pretty difficult. At that point we decided that the car was haunted. Someone was most likely killed in it in a shootout. We made the decision to trade it in.

Meanwhile Dad tied the passenger door shut with a heavy rope, winding it around the seat and through the door handle. He was following me home when just in front of the little church near the center of town, the door flew open, rope and all. There is a cemetery behind the church.

That was our last encounter with our ghost, because the car was sold an hour later for $650 (another bargain). We never heard any more about the 1952 Ford, and I never saw it again. Perhaps the ghost had had its last ride.

SÉANCE

B. ELAINE STORY

White candles were lit to keep bad spirits from intruding, and black plastic had been taped over the windows. With the exception of a few curious newcomers, everyone expected nothing less than communication with the dead. Each progressive séance had produced enough coincidences to make even a doubting Thomas a believer.

The room was filled with teenagers. News had spread around town, and parties that had started out as typical teenage get-togethers, with the added fascination of the supernatural as entertainment, had become so intriguing and so mystifying that no one wanted to stop the séances until much more had been accomplished. After all, everyone was just having fun.

On this particular night, the group decided to "call back" a guy named Nicky, who had died a few years earlier from leukemia at the age of twenty-seven. He really had no claim to fame—he simply happened to be dead. He had been friends with some members of the audience, and almost everyone else had known him or knew of him, because we lived in a small town.

The main practitioners of the séance placed their hands on the Ouija board's dial. Different kids from the crowd asked questions; the first few were simple and factual: "What was your wife's name?" "What year did you graduate from high school?" The few people who knew Nicky well posed questions of a more specific nature, with answers only the questioner would know. Every question was answered correctly and was followed by a silence from the amazed audience. One skeptic asked Nicky to give a physical sign as evidence that a connection had truly been made. The Ouija dial spelled out that they would receive a sign at midnight, and hands jerked away from the board as people looked at each other with eyes sick with the joy of fear. A certain energy was shared by all in the room, an energy that bound them together.

At midnight, the sound of a loud, rumbling motorcycle racing down the street outside broke the silence. The teenagers scrambled out of their chairs and rushed to the windows, but no one saw a bike.

"That was a Harley-Davidson. Nicky owned the baddest Harley in the county." We checked each other's facial expressions. Some of the girls unconsciously covered their mouths with their hands. Others tried to offer some logical explanation to ears already prejudiced against reason. What they all had witnessed through sight and sound was all they needed to satisfy the obvious conclusion, even if the obvious was beyond explanation.

Still, one determined guest had to make it vocal. "Ask it if that was Nicky's bike."

No one was surprised when the Ouija dial flew upward to "yes." The dial then started moving without the prompting of a question and began to spell out this message: "Meet me at my grave."

For some this was too much to consider, but for most it was an invitation too "Poesque" to refuse. It was as if the final answer lay at the Concord Methodist Churchyard.

Few hesitated to jump into their cars and drive the eight miles across narrow, winding roads to the destination suggested by the Ouija. Upon arrival at the cemetery, the crowd set out for Nicky's grave. Even though it was midsummer, there was something chilling in the damp, foggy air, something that lashed their faces and whispered in their ears. The incessant sound of crickets became a monotonous torment as no one dared to utter a sound, given the solemnity of their purpose. When the first group came within sight of the grave, they froze in their steps, either from disbelief or from facing cold reality. No one came within twenty feet of Nicky's final resting place, because those who looked through the moonlit haze saw a dim, shadowy figure sitting on Nicky's tombstone, arms outstretched to greet them. They ran back to their cars, slipping on wet grass, panting, their hearts pounding.

Days later, the parents of some of the kids casually remarked how strange it was that they had seen a tall, thin man walking down Chapel Avenue around midnight, wearing a gray pin-striped suit.

Nicky had been buried in a gray pin-striped suit.

NIGHTLY RITUAL

KATHLEEN TAYLOR

They say there are no such things as ghosts, but we sometimes wonder why incidents such as those I am about to relate occur.

When I was eight years old, my mother saw a man standing in our kitchen at about one o'clock every morning. He would slowly remove his suit coat, put it on a hanger, and hang it on the dish closet door. My parents' bedroom was off the kitchen, and she could see the dish closet from her bed. After a few nights of viewing this ritual, she told my father that she was seeing someone in the kitchen every night. She would not tell him what the man was doing; she insisted instead that the next night she would wake my father to see whether he saw anything and, if he did see something, to describe what it was.

When the man next appeared, my mother poked my father to wake him. The two of them sat up in bed and watched the man go through his nightly motions. My father related to my mother exactly what he saw— the same thing she had been witnessing for several nights.

The next day my mother told her aunt, who lived downstairs in the same house, about seeing the man. Her aunt had seen him, too, and her description of him fit perfectly. My great-aunt said that this man had lived in our rooms before we moved in. It seems he used to work from 4:00 p.m. until midnight and got home from work each night about 1:00 a.m., the same time that my mother was seeing the apparition. She further added that he always hung his coat on the dish closet door instead of in the bedroom so as not to disturb his wife. She told my mother that she had heard that his ashes were still somewhere in our rooms.

For quite some time my mother and father continued to see the man and learned not to let him bother them. One day my mother was cleaning the living room windows and curtains—she had taken down the shades—and was sitting on the couch talking to her cousin. They saw the sunlight from the bare windows shining into the open metal grillwork on the front panel of the old fireplace. My mother thought that there was dust in the fireplace and took off the metal panel and swept it out. After this was done, the man never appeared again. My mother finally realized that she had found his ashes—it hadn't been dust in the fireplace after all.

A HOUSE IN THE WOODS

NAN ROWE

As they crept through the dense brush, the two girls clung tightly to each other. The fear and excitement growing within them threatened to burst forth in nervous giggles. They had talked of nothing but this adventure for a month. Since the day they had unexpectedly discovered the little house in the woods about a mile from their grandparents' farm, they had been anticipating this daring odyssey. They just knew the place was haunted. They wanted to explore the interior yet dreaded what they might find (or what might find them).

When they had first come upon the house, they had run away from it. With faces and hands scratched and burrs all over their socks, they had breathlessly arrived home only to wish that they had stayed and explored their discovery. They had heard a noise upstairs and had not made it past the front porch.

Cathy had just celebrated her fourteenth birthday. Somehow she felt that her childhood was vanishing, and she desperately wanted one great adventure to tuck into her memory before she headed down the path to adulthood. It had taken a lot of begging, from both Cathy and twelve-year-old Nan, to convince their parents to allow them to visit the farm a second time that summer. The drive from the city was a long one, and their parents were always so busy. But the girls were persistent and were finally granted their wish.

Their eyes round with fear, their hearts pounding, the youngsters walked slowly, hands gripping each others' shoulders, until they were within a few feet of the building. They peered out from behind a large tree, afraid to continue. The wind blew softly and branches scraped the old metal roof. A rabbit, disturbed by their presence, scurried away. The girls winced but held their ground. They were determined to go inside this time.

What once must have been a lovely little home had become a crumbling shack. The years had not been kind. The shutters dangled precariously from rusty nails, most of the window glass was broken, and the front door stood halfway open. Grass and weeds grew between the floorboards of what was once a fine little porch.

The anxious visitors ventured forward and shakily entered the doorway. Cathy softly called out, "Is anyone home?" and immediately burst out laughing at the thought of anyone inhabiting this hovel. Nan crept slowly behind her sister, wishing she was anywhere but in this horrible house. The living room furniture, once polished and attractive, was dry and dusty. The couch sagged and the chairs gave off a musty odor, stuffing coming out of every seam. Old magazines lay soiled and torn on the floor.

From room to room the girls crept, eyes wide, ears sensitive to every sigh the lonely old house issued. The hallway was filthy with dust, and there were large holes in the floor around which the visitors stepped carefully. As they entered the kitchen, they experienced a very peculiar feeling—a sensation that they were not alone, that they were being watched. An old wooden table stood forlornly in the center of the room. On top of the table was a dinner setting. It looked almost as if someone had been dining and had been interrupted. A chair was partially pulled out from the table. Over the plate, black food remnants remained. The fork was still there, along with a chipped, stained coffee cup. A corroded sugar bowl, a saltshaker, and a napkin holder sat desolately in the middle of that old table. Feeling very uncomfortable, the pair fled the room and began to ascend the stairway to the second floor.

Testing each step as they climbed, they ventured slowly up toward the dark rooms. A torn shade hung sideways on the window straight ahead of them, allowing just a little sunlight to brighten their path. Bees flew in and out of the broken panes. As they reached the second floor the peculiar feeling returned—were they being watched? Covered with goose bumps, neither voiced the fear, hoping it was just nerves.

Quickening their pace they entered the first room they came to. What should have been a very pretty brass bed stood in the corner, an old, filthy patchwork quilt on it. There was a mirrored dressing table upon which a rusty metal hairbrush and a broken vase sat. The mirror was cracked and had turned a gold color. The girls' reflections were distorted, barely recognizable. In one corner several cardboard boxes had decomposed and the box fragments and their contents had formed a small, smelly heap on the stained linoleum, which was cracked and peeling away from the floor. The offensive odor drove them from the room and into the other one across the hall.

The first to enter, Cathy made a guttural sound and her hand flew to her mouth. Hearing it, Nan stopped dead in her tracks until her sister slowly motioned her in. They were both stunned. An old wooden rocking horse in the middle of that room was rocking back and forth. It was going fast, as if a child had just hopped off. Their knees felt weak. Someone was in there with them! Neither girl moved. Time seemed to stand still as the horse slowed its motion and finally stopped altogether.

They began to survey the room and were surprised to note that there was no dust. The room was neat. The wood floor shone and the scatter rug, although worn, was clean and fresh. An enormous trunk, similar to the treasure chests they had often read about, sat by one wall. An ancient treadle sewing machine was near it. As they looked around they noticed an old, rather primitive baby stroller and a very old rocking chair. A baby crib, with a stained mattress, occupied one corner of the room. A long, narrow mirror was nailed to the back of a door. The mirror was cracked and yellowed, but the reflections were remarkably clear. The sheer curtains, in shreds, were not moving. As a matter of fact, not even a small breeze was blowing through the broken windowpanes—yet the rocking horse had been rocking.

After what seemed like ages, Nan felt her fear subsiding slightly and her curiosity returning. Of like minds, the sisters crept silently toward the chest. Very deliberately, Cathy lifted the lid and kneeled on the floor. Nan joined her and they enjoyed a most wonderful discovery. The ancient repository held many old letters and photographs. Temporarily ignoring the rocking horse, the trespassers were transported back in time as they examined the pictures. As they began to read the letters, they found that they had to strain their eyes and even improvise a little, as the ink had faded and smeared. Obviously written during a war by a weary soldier to the woman he loved, the letters contained a tiny piece of history. Although the snooping girls felt a little guilty for their invasion of privacy, the remorse was not heavy enough to stop them. The words on the stained, faded paper were from the heart. He had missed her so much. He was so afraid he would die and never see her again. He had received the pictures of their little son and was amazed at how much he had changed. Why was he so thin?

Cathy and Nan imagined that the man who had last lived in this house was once a young soldier who had written those letters to his lady love. The sisters took turns reading them aloud to each other. Cathy began reading a letter written in a woman's handwriting. She read it aloud in the beginning, but soon began to read silently as tears slipped down her cheeks. Nan kept asking her what was wrong, but Cathy was not to be interrupted. When she had finished, she handed the epistle to her sister. Evidently, the soldier's wife had written the agonizing words to inform him of their little son's tragic death. At the age of three, he had developed pneumonia and passed away.

The joy of finding the pictures and letters ebbed as the girls became emotionally involved in the anguish this couple must have faced. Cathy sadly reached into the trunk and withdrew a yellowed and very dry folded parchment. As she opened it the parchment fell apart where it had been folded. Piecing it together, she realized it was a very old telegram. It stated simply that the soldier's wife was dead—she had taken her own life. That poor man. First his son and then his wife. Nan placed the pieces on her lap as she read the words in the strange, large type, unconsciously smoothing the pieces of paper with the palm of her hand.

Without speaking, the unhappy pair placed everything back into the old chest, closed the top, and stood up to leave. They had no right to be there. They wanted to go home. As they headed toward the door, they both glanced at the old rocking horse. It was still, but at that very moment the rocking chair began to move slowly back and forth. Neither of them could move a muscle. Then to their utter astonishment they heard soft humming—the nearly inaudible humming of a lullaby. Cathy had difficulty breathing. An involuntary swallow caused a gulping sound to escape her lips. Nan felt she was paralyzed. She willed her legs to run, but they would not obey.

Unaware that they were clinging to each other, the trembling girls began to move sideways toward the open door. Their eyes darted from the rocking chair to the door. As they slithered past the closet, Nan groaned. It was an awful animal sound, and Cathy grabbed her as she fell to her knees. Nan pointed to the door mirror as she sat slumped and panting for air. Cathy followed her gaze to the mirror and her stunned expression confirmed that she saw it too. There was a lovely lady sitting in the rocking chair holding a small child on her lap. The pair slowly looked back at the rocking chair. It was empty! Only the mirrored reflection revealed the image of the woman, who looked content and absolutely peaceful. Her eyes never left them.

On their feet in seconds, fleeing in total terror, the sisters went down the steps three at a time. Leaping through the front doorway and over the front porch, they ran like frightened deer until they could no longer control their legs. They collapsed under a big tree, gulping huge mouthfuls of fresh air. The house was out of sight, the birds were singing, and bees droned around them.

Oddly, neither girl wept. They wanted to but somehow felt that it would be childish, and they were not children anymore. They did not doubt their sanity. They knew what they had seen. It had been real. They were still terrified. They felt older than they ever had in their entire lives.

Cathy and Nan left their ghost and her little child alone with the serenity they had found. The girls told no one. It was their lifelong secret. Who would have believed them anyway?

PINK LADY

JUDY TUSCHAK

You asked for it! I thought I'd have to go to my grave with the story untold, but no! Please allow me to begin at the beginning, with my husband, Tom.

By day he is a highly regarded educator, an entirely sane, responsible, and caring person dedicated to protecting and enriching the lives of those he loves.

At night, however, a darker aspect of his personality surfaces. He somnambulates. He drives me crazy running around the house from room to room, opening and closing whatever he's driven to open or close, talking to only he knows whom.

Sometimes he even somnambuLAYS, which is to say that he does similar but not matchingly odd things without even leaving our bed. He sits upright with arms outstretched like a mummy or leans over me in a stance like a vulture's, eyes wide and staring, uttering not a sound.

So it's not that I'm unused to that certain sensation indicating a strange otherworldly presence nearby. In fact, I'd like to think that I'm better prepared than most to deal with such eventualities because, thanks to Tom, I have a method. I've learned to will myself to be calm; I remain still and open my eyes very slowly so as not to startle him when I sense his goings-on.

It works for us.

And it worked for the ghost.

There were no untoward sounds, no padding feet, no doors or windows creaking, no unearthly rush of wind on that chill February evening in 1972, but I awoke slowly, sensing the dead air that hangs unnaturally between two still and opposite bodies.

I expected to see the unfocused stare of my mustachioed Ukrainian lovemonster hovering over me like Dr. Frankenstein's creation, but instead, floating serenely above our bed, was the top half only of a young, attractive blond woman wearing a pale pink, short-sleeved angora sweater and a discreet pearl choker. She was holding a Kodak Instamatic camera at the ready. She appeared to be taking pictures of Tom as he slept. Strangely enough, there was no sensation of fear attached to this phenomenon. Wide-eyed surprise, disbelief, attraction—yes. In fact, I forced myself to blink hard, twice, in an attempt to dissolve the image. I even pinched my leg quietly under the covers to assure myself I wasn't dreaming. It hurt!

Meanwhile, she continued to click away, finally widening her frame to include me. Looking at her I felt happy knowing that she cared enough to want to know Tom better, wanted to know us together.

After all, she had died two years before he and I had even met.

The fact that this apparition didn't resemble my American Indian mother in the slightest (she was considerably younger than Mom had been at her death in 1961) and that we hadn't exchanged a single word between us did not alter my perception that this was indeed she, that she was truly here, and that she cared about me, about Tom, about us.

At peace, I finally closed my eyes to rest a moment, and she disappeared. Brief disappointment quickly gave way to giddy excitement as I replayed the strange encounter in my mind. I felt I had to share it and a drowsy, skeptical Tom was kind enough to let me recount the whole thing, twice, before he drifted back to sleep.

I lay in bed quietly considering the wonder and the improbability of it all until I too slept.

In the light of morning I still felt the charm of the dream, but recognized that that was what it must have been, a dream. I shook my head as I recalled the surety I'd felt that that presence, so unlike my mom in life, was so certainly she in the afterlife.

Of course, it was absurd.

But, oh, it felt so real!

There were stirrings upstairs. I could hear the baby, Suzy, pounding on the top bar of her crib. I called to the girls as I mounted the double bank of steps, greeting them with lively hellos and the good news of a bright, crisp, sunny day ready to meet us.

I hugged Suzy over the bars, chatting as I moved from girl to girl. Amy awoke gently as I kissed her big-girl ear.

Beckie was still sound asleep as I approached, the comforter pulled up to within an inch of her tiny nose. I smoothed aside her strawberry bangs to waken her by whispering "Little Bugs" but, abruptly, she sat right up, her amber eyes bright, their golden flecks on fire.

"Is she still here?" she asked with feverish excitement.

"What, Beck?"

"Is she still here?" she demanded, her breathless little voice exasperated that I hadn't understood her the first time.

"Who?" I asked innocently, without a shadow of foreboding.

"The pink lady. The pink lady from last night. Is she still here? She said she'd stay."

Bring up the "Twilight Zone" theme please!

THE FLOATING HEAD

LUCILLE CIAPPINA

The scene is the small town where I grew up. We had never owned our own home, so moving from time to time was part of our family pattern.

When I was twelve, we lived adjacent to a huge cemetery. Strangely, nothing ever happened there. At one point, when I was older, we once again found reason to switch residences. The new apartment, close to the downtown area, was the first floor of an old mansion. It boasted an enormous front parlor with floor-to-ceiling bay windows, and this room served as my bedroom. Without question, as I was the only girl in the family, the best bedroom was always mine. In this apartment, my two brothers shared one of the two small bedrooms; my parents shared the other. I was to pay the price for being so spoiled.

We had not lived there long before discovering that we had acquired a very abusive landlord, who, unfortunately, also had the apartment over us. My parents, realizing that moving here had been a mistake, began talk of packing up once again. One of our relatives got us a place in a building that he lived in, but we could not move in right away.

My room unnerved me a bit. Although I felt queenly in its spaciousness, it was in an area by itself, separated from the rest of the bedrooms by a large living room and also a long hallway. Each night, I would turn off the lamp by my bed, scan the black doorway, which faced me, and pull the covers over my head.

One night I awoke from a deep sleep with a start. There, at the upper part of that pitch-black doorway, hung the head of a man. No body, just a head. I *was* awake, and it did *not* go away! I can still describe the exact picture. The head was that of an old man. His face was round, his hair had receded, and he boasted a huge white mustache. His head was illuminated by something that was bright red, as though it was lit up from behind by fire. He was smiling at me. The head just stayed there, and I froze.

My trembling hand reached for the light. In the brightness of the room, he was gone. After a while, I raised all the blinds in the bay windows and turned off the light. The streetlights filled the room, and I pulled the blankets tight about me and somehow went back to sleep.

But my visions were not so easily put to rest. Sometime thereafter, I awoke again. I looked up and there, bending *over* me, was a very heavy-set older woman. She was staring down at me in a very curious way, as though she did not know me. My hand went for that lamp. I felt it was going right through her.

I slept no more. The light went out no more. And I never slept in that room again. I stayed with an aunt until we finally moved. My mother told me that she was greatly relieved herself that we were moving out because I had described in perfect detail the older couple that, when she was a girl, was known to live here. According to her beliefs, the old folks had come to search for their daughter (of which they had one) to ask for prayers. Well, for those who may believe even faintly in hell, the man's face *had* been lit by fire!

Good night!

THE BLUE HOUSEDRESS

VIRGINIA STONE

It was a warm, sultry summer evening in 1943 and my father, a young boy, was disturbed in his sleep. He opened his eyes and peeped over the edge of his covers. He knew it was late because he could not hear any of his family moving around or talking downstairs. He glanced at the window where a slight breeze was rustling the sheer draperies of his bedroom. The old, three-story house creaked in familiar ways, and, with a sigh, Jimmy rolled over to go back to sleep.

Suddenly, something made him look toward the doorway. Standing on the threshold was the figure of a woman wearing his mother's favorite blue housedress. Startled, he called out, "Mother!" There was no answer. The figure did not move. At this, Jimmy dived under his sheet and trembled with fright. Then, to his horror, he felt a slight pressure on the edge of his bed, as if someone had sat down on the corner. After this moment my father remembered nothing until he awoke to see the sunlight streaming into his room the next morning.

Jimmy ran downstairs to tell his parents about what he had encountered during the night. He frantically told his father about the figure in the doorway. My grandfather just laughed and continued with his breakfast. Jimmy approached his mother and asked whether she had entered his bedroom the previous night. After all, the figure was wearing her blue housedress. My grandmother assured my father that she certainly was not the mysterious figure in the doorway.

Throughout breakfast my father was silent and barely touched his food. He knew he had not dreamed the episode. It was very real, and yet no one believed him.

After breakfast my grandmother took my father upstairs to her large walk-in closet on the third floor. She wanted to reassure her son that he had in fact dreamed the entire scene. She would prove this by finding her blue housedress. She was confident that this would ease Jimmy's mind.

Upstairs both my father and my grandmother rummaged through the large closet. They checked every clothing hanger and hook. The blue housedress had vanished.

To this day my grandmother has never found her housedress and my father has never learned the identity of the mysterious visitor.

A WOMAN IN THE WELL

SARAH M. BRANGAN

I'm fourteen years old and not afraid of ghosts, I never have nightmares, and no one has ever accused me of having an overactive imagination. But I did have one experience that I can't explain. I have never told anyone about it, and I have never before written it down. I did, however, make a couple of brief entries in my diary. Believe it or not, I have kept a diary since I was five years old. The entries I made in August 1983, when I was seven, have given me the sequence of events for this account.

We lived on top of a steep hill near a small town. Behind our house there were miles of woods and hills, then a line of trees where a hay field started. It was a mile farther past that to the first back road. So you can see we lived way out in the country, and it was scenic and quiet.

My dad used to make a big deal out of taking my younger sister Emily and me for a hike. We would pack peanut-butter crackers, sodas, potato chips, and whatever else we wanted into a backpack and set off out the back door into the woods. Dad would take a knife on his belt, just in case. We also carried rusty penknives and a compass. We usually took a camera and a bag to collect things in.

When we were about fifty feet into the woods, when we could no longer see our house, we might as well have been in the wilds of Alaska. Everything was interesting. We probably walked for about a quarter of a mile before we looked for a place to break out the food. After we had eaten, we would look for "stuff." We would collect giant toadstools, feathers, acorns, special rocks, and items like that. Dad carried the bag.

One day we realized we were in the middle of an apple orchard. There were apple trees all around and tons of apples on the ground. There were several kinds of other trees mixed in, and the apple trees looked old and not very healthy. We had been this way many times before but had never noticed what was obviously an orchard.

We hiked a little farther, around the side of a steep hill, and noticed a pipe running along the ground. It was an iron pipe, very rusty, and kind of buried in the leaves, visible just here and there. It ran up the hill, more or less in the direction of where we had eaten our lunch.

Dad made a game of tracing the pipe; he really didn't know what to make of it himself. We followed it down to the bottom of the hill, where it ended at a flat place. We saw nothing special there.

Then it was time to go back—I guess we had been out for about an hour or so—and we followed the pipe back up the hill. Finally we lost it again, but we continued to walk in the direction the pipe was pointing. Near the top of the hill we came to a round pile of flat rocks about two feet high and about six feet in diameter. It was a well.

The entire inside of the well was lined with flat stone, and it was deep. Dad said it was fifteen feet deep, maybe more. If you looked over one side you could see a reflection of your face way down there in the water. We dropped some stones into the water, and Dad took some pictures of our reflections. He said that an open well was dangerous, and he wondered why no one had covered it over.

We sat on the edge of the well, one on either side of Dad, and finished the crackers and soda we had saved for the hike back. While I was eating I looked down at my reflection and dropped small stones in the water to make rings. When the ripples stopped, my reflection would be crystal-clear again.

But one time it wasn't. When the water became calm it wasn't myself that I saw looking up at me. I must have made a noise or a gasp because Dad looked at me and told me to be careful.

I looked back down, and there it was again. I looked at Emily. She was looking into the well, but she didn't seem very interested. I could tell that she was looking at her own reflection. But what I saw was an elderly woman.

She had white frizzy hair, and she was extremely skinny. She had the kind of neck where the bones stick out. She looked content. I mean, she wasn't screaming or scary or anything. I looked around and saw that there was no reason for that reflection to be there. There were just the three of us.

I looked back down; the woman was still there. Then I heard a voice in my head say, "You've got the same initials as I do, Sarah." Emily then dropped another stone into the well, and when the ripples stopped, the woman was gone.

I think it must have happened pretty quickly—maybe the whole thing took only a minute or so, I don't know for sure. I didn't drop any more stones into the well. In fact, I didn't look for the reflection again.

I didn't say anything about the incident to anyone. At the time I didn't think it was anything more than something unusual I saw on one of our hikes.

A month later, I woke up for some reason during the night and there she was again, the same woman. She was wearing a white apron and, in my head, I heard her say, "When you come back to visit me again, Sarah, be careful around the well." She was just standing there at the foot of my bed. Even though she didn't say so, I knew she was the owner or the wife of the owner of the orchard. Even after she had faded away, I could smell apples.

She seemed at peace and kind, and I wasn't afraid. She might have been there for about a minute, and then she faded away. That was the last I ever saw of her. We never hiked in the direction of the well again, and about a year later we moved to another town not too far away.

I guess there are ways to research just who owned the property years ago, and I know I will some day. I bet that someone with my initials lived there in a house that was torn down about a hundred years ago. Maybe she knew what she was talking about when she told me to be careful by the well.

DID I LOCK THE BASEMENT DOOR?

LAURA GIANNONE

On a cold snowy night I was curled up on my sofa watching television, waiting for my husband to come home from work. My two babies were upstairs, asleep in their cribs.

We'd just moved into the middle apartment of a seven-family row house. I was so proud of my new home.

The downstairs consisted of the living room, dining room, and kitchen, all in a row. A house with this layout is often called a shotgun house, because a gun, shot through the front door, would send a bullet right through to the back door.

Each of the three rooms downstairs had a door: the living room had the front door; the kitchen had the back door; and the center room, which I used as a dining room, had a door to the basement. Even the basement had a door that led to the outside.

The apartment had been the scene of a gruesome murder-suicide. It seems that the lady of the house, who used the center room as a den, was shot dead by her husband one day as she watched television.

In the quiet of that night I slowly became aware of heavy footsteps deliberately climbing the stairs from the basement. My first thought was that some patient had escaped from the nearby mental hospital. Had I locked the basement door? We had no phone yet. My babies were upstairs, defenseless, except for me. I grabbed the nearest heavy object, a bookend, and waited for someone to open the door to the basement.

The footsteps reached the top of the stairs, the doorknob turned slowly, but the door did not open. I felt as if time stood still. My fear blocked out all sounds, and I could hear only my heart pounding like a bass drum. My arms ached from holding the bookend above my head.

Finally I couldn't stand it anymore. With one hand, I held the bookend, and with the other I reached over and yanked open the door. It had been unlocked. No one was there. No snowy footprints on the stairs. I ran down and opened the door that led outside. No footprints in the snow either.

The next day I told the story to my neighbor, who had lived next door when the previous tenant shot his wife and then himself. I laughed and said, "Boy, am I glad I know he came in through the kitchen door."

"Oh, no," she replied, "he came up the basement stairs."

AN UNEXPECTED PASSENGER

JUDY SNYDER

One fine summer evening when I was sixteen, I was visiting my friend Sarah, whose mother was a devout believer in spirits. It was only natural that the conversation turned in that direction. At one point when my friend and I had gone into the kitchen to make lemonade, Sarah asked me what I believed. I told her that I really wasn't sure, and then, as if on cue, a small portable fan clicked on, seemingly of its own accord.

Sarah was still standing at the sink some distance from the fan, making the lemonade. "Oh, it's just Bill," she said as she carried the pitcher to the table. "Bill, turn it off!" Off went the fan. I've always prided myself on my ability to be logical, and I thought that the fan must have had some type of short in it and that Sarah really had the timing down on her joke. I decided to let it pass as we sat down with large glasses of the tart drink.

Later I asked Sarah about Bill, and I was told that he was one of the ghosts that resided in the house. It seems, she explained, that several spirits had adopted her family. Bill was playful and evidently liked me and wanted to be introduced. I think I gave an intelligent reply such as "Uh-huh," which surely suggested that I thought it was some sort of joke. But at my insistence Sarah began to tell me a little bit about the others who shared their home. Perhaps Bill didn't appreciate my disbelief, because odd things started to happen. I had put my glass down after taking a few sips, and when I reached for it, it had been moved about three inches away from the spot where I'd placed it. Logic told me that Sarah could have secretly tugged on the tablecloth, thereby moving the glass, but then my glass actually slid toward me—as I watched. Nothing else on the table moved. That pretty much killed my parlor-trick theory.

By this time Mrs. Reynolds had joined us, and, when the fan began flicking on and off again, it was she who admonished Bill, asking him whether he intended to frighten me or whether he didn't want me to like him. After that he behaved himself, and the discussion continued until a fairly late hour. Mrs. Reynolds believed that we are surrounded by spirits all of the time and that, with a few exceptions, they are really quite helpful.

As I got ready to leave, Sarah asked me to call her when I arrived home so that they would know I'd had a safe journey. I agreed. Soon I turned my Ford Gremlin toward home.

Although I was still perplexed about Sarah's ghosts, I put them out of my mind and concentrated on driving. I had turned on the radio and was singing along with it when I glanced into the rearview mirror. A startled sound escaped from me because there in the mirror I saw what appeared to be an American Indian! He had a strong, dark face with a hooked nose, his mouth a straight line. His hair was dark and appeared shoulder length, and he had a band around his head. His body seemed to be wrapped in a coarse blanket. I don't remember thinking about what to do; I just acted. Swerving off the road, I jammed on the brakes and shifted into park, while simultaneously throwing open my door. I half fell, half jumped, out onto the street; my one conscious thought was to put distance between myself and the uninvited passenger. As my feet hit the pavement, I was turned partially and looked into the backseat. There was no one there! Since my door was still gaping open, the interior was bathed in the courtesy light's glow. A Gremlin is a very small car, and there was no room for him to hide. There simply was no one there.

Moments passed while I tried to think of a logical explanation and of what to do next. If I abandoned my car for something I'd imagined, I'd be ridiculed. I decided, however, that if he appeared again I would definitely leave the car and walk home.

I had just entered my parents' house when the phone rang. I remembered promising Sarah I would call and wasn't surprised that she was on the other end of the line. By now, I had more or less convinced myself that I had one heck of an imagination and that I shouldn't tell anyone about my "apparition." But here was Sarah saying, "Red Feather says he's sorry that he frightened you. I sent him to be sure you got home okay."

There is no logical explanation of how Sarah could have known that I'd had a passenger. Unless, of course, she had conversed with a ghost.

OLD LINENS AND LACE

SANDY GEISER

It started out like any other Sunday morning. My girlfriend and I were setting out early for the annual antiques fair in a neighboring town. There was a chill in the air—quite unusual for August—and the morning breeze sent shivers down my spine.

When we pulled into the parking area, we noticed that there were already tons of people milling around. The sun was starting to peek out from behind the clouds, warming me up a little.

I was looking for an antique trunk in which to store my assorted collection of old linens and lace. I've always been intrigued by old things, and my collection had grown to the point that I needed more storage space.

As we walked around I spotted a small trunk with rusted hinges over in a corner behind a box of old books and magazines. As I approached it to have a closer look, I could see that the lid was open enough to reveal some linens inside. "Just perfect," I thought to myself. "Just what I've been looking for, and it's even filled with old linens and lace. This is too good to be true."

I opened the lid the rest of the way and started pulling out an array of lace collars, gloves, doilies, and tablecloths. They were in beautiful condition, and you could tell that whoever had once owned them had taken great pride in them. I was truly elated at my find. I couldn't wait to get the trunk and its contents home.

Upon arriving home I gently laundered all the delicate pieces and hung them outside to dry. They had been so yellow when I started to launder them that I didn't think they'd ever come clean, but the late afternoon sun bleached everything a beautiful white, a white that these articles hadn't seen in years. To my surprise everything looked absolutely new, and every piece had that marvelous outdoor smell that things get from hanging outside. I carefully took them down from the clothesline and brought them inside to press them.

As I was finishing the last lace collar, folding it before I put it into the trunk, I felt that strange cold breeze that I had felt that morning. I thought to myself, "How strange for a hot August night." But I quickly forgot all about it as I headed upstairs and drew my bath. I stepped into the tub and slowly eased myself into a reclining position. The water quickly surrounded my entire body, and I felt the heat penetrate through my skin and warm me internally.

It was around midnight when I finally settled into bed. I pulled the sheets up under my chin and felt sleep taking over. At precisely 3:00 a.m. (I remember the time because I heard the clock downstairs chime three), it happened. I heard a soft, quiet voice speaking to me in the darkness of my room. She was floating like a cloud over my bed, and I could vaguely make out the silhouette of her body.

She told me her name was Wanda May Wilson and that she had died at an early age. She said that her spirit had been staying in the trunk that I had bought yesterday and that all the laces had belonged to her. She said she had watched how gently I had washed and ironed all her linens. She could tell I must be a very loving person.

"I've been waiting for a long time," she said, "for the right person, and I feel that you're the one." I had no idea what she was talking about. The strange breeze that I had felt the day before had returned, and I could feel her presence getting closer and closer. By that time I understood what she meant. She wanted my body for her soul. "Please," she begged, "I never had a chance at life and you're my chance; please let me live my life again!"

I started screaming. My cries woke up my husband, who had been sound asleep next to me. Startled, he sat straight up in bed. He asked me what had happened, and when I told him he said it was only a dream. "No!" I insisted. "It was real, I know it was."

To this day I feel that I actually had contact with the hereafter.

TOMBSTONE DREAMS

DEE MYERS

One evening in the early 1980s when I was thirty-five years old and living with my two young daughters in the Baltimore suburbs, I had a very realistic dream. All of a sudden I was above my sleeping body and pulled outside of my room and out of the house. I didn't know where I was going and had no control over my destination. A force was moving me fast and low to the ground. I could clearly see various landmarks—homes, stores, and street signs—as I was being whisked to God knows where. Because I was so close to the ground, I could almost touch the gravel in the road. After making a few turns, I found myself in an old cemetery. There were many tombstones—some with statues atop them, others in various shapes.

I was being pulled to one specific area, where I felt I was being sucked down into the grass over a specific grave. I saw the name on the stone and dates of birth and death. This sucking, this smothering feeling, was all too real. As I was being pressed closer to the dirt, I rebelled.

Suddenly I was back in my bed. I sat up shaking, the memory of what had just happened very clear. It took some time before I returned to sleep that night, and I wrote the experience off as a bad dream.

But the dream stayed with me during the next few days. The feeling was so intense, so real. When Saturday rolled around, I thought I'd try to follow those landmarks, to see if things "clicked." I suggested to my girls that we take a mystery ride. Saturday was a good day to have an adventure. It was early spring, and we packed up some snacks. "Let's take King (our faithful dog)," I said, and I started the car, which we called Nelly.

The kids were in high spirits, King was hanging out the window, and I was intently looking for those landmarks. Quietly I made the proper turns, passing one site after another. Yes, at each mile, tree, or sign the dream was becoming more real. I didn't feel too good about the reality, but I felt safe—sunny spring day, music, kids, dog.

I guess I was getting quieter, thinking about where this terrible dream had ended, but I had to prove that it wasn't real. But then we came upon the main entrance to the city's oldest cemetery. The gates were open and we drove in. Everything was just as it had been in the dream, and I knew exactly where I was going. By now, my kids were really perplexed, but I told them that we were only going to be here a short time, looking at the old gravestones.

We came to the place. I knew it was *the* place. Three tall bushes were the last landmark; the gravestone was in front of them. The girls and dog jumped out of the car and began to roam around freely. I was a little slower. I walked to those tall bushes; on the ground in front of them was only a lot of dead grass. I kicked the clippings around. I saw nothing, and I was relieved even though a storm was approaching in the distance.

Just then, one of my girls called me over to see a unique photograph on a tombstone. While I was distracted, King wandered over to the site I had been examining. I turned around to find the dog digging up the loose grass and dirt in front of the bushes. There *was* an old tombstone under there! I went over and knelt down to help remove the debris. There was the name, then the dates. The same name and dates that I had seen in my dream.

I was immediately chilled. Who was this girl? Why did she die so young, at eighteen? Why was I selected to travel to her grave site? Why had I been forcibly pulled to her?

I packed up the kids and dog and went home. As the rainstorm hit our area, I was fearful. I told no one what had happened. My mind has blanked out her full name—but her first name is Elizabeth. I don't want to think too much about it. I know where she is.

Ten years later she still haunts me. Should I go back? Is there something I need to tell her? The story is real—but somehow unfinished. And I'm afraid to go back there alone.

THE NEGATIVE

MARLYS DREWS

In 1966 my four sons and I moved to a new house in Seattle. The house sat high on the side of a hill, and afforded us a beautiful view of Puget Sound. It had three stories—bedrooms on the second floor, a living area on the main floor, and two bedrooms in the basement, where three of my sons slept.

One night, June 27, to be exact, I was asleep upstairs. My youngest son was asleep in the adjoining room. At 12:20 a.m., I heard someone call me from the bottom of the stairs. I woke up, looked at the clock, and listened to the footsteps on the stairs. When I heard the footsteps, I got out of bed immediately because I thought one of the boys was sick and needed help. I quietly went down the steps to the main floor, and found the door at the bottom of the stairs open. I was surprised to find the door open, because I always made sure it was closed when I went to bed. I called to the boys, but got no answer. But I was still convinced I'd heard one of my sons.

I went through the kitchen to the basement, quietly asking the boys what was wrong. I found them all fast asleep. I couldn't figure this out. I went back upstairs and walked through the house to the living room. I even went out on the front steps to see whether anyone was there. Nobody.

I wasn't frightened but curious about what had awakened me. As I looked out the window, I had a strange sense of peacefulness. I remember thinking to myself that whoever it was who had called me was satisfied that I had heard the call.

The next morning I telephoned a close friend of mine who was psychic and told her of my late-night experience. She didn't say anything for a while, and then she started talking very slowly, asking me whether there was an attic in the house. I told her that there wasn't, but that there was a storage area upstairs under the eaves. She asked me whether it was finished off inside, and I told her it wasn't. She told me to go up and look by a rafter that came down to the floor. There I would find a picture. I told her I would call her back after I made my search.

I went up to the storage area with a flashlight. I searched near the rafters, as she had instructed, and was surprised to find a negative stuck at the base of one of them. I called her right back and told her what I had found. She said that she had a strong feeling that there was a woman in the picture, and that she was the one who had awakened me. There was indeed a woman in the picture, with two small children standing on either side of her. By the woman's clothes and hairstyle, I knew that the picture had been taken in the 1940s.

My friend suggested that I find out more about the previous owners. I had the negative printed and then took it to the next-door neighbors, who had lived there many years.

The neighbors told me that the original owners of my house were an Italian couple with two children, a boy and a girl. The children grew up there, and the daughter married a merchant seaman. When her husband was at sea, she and her two children would stay with her parents.

Always she would stand at the window and watch the ships come and go, hoping to see her husband's ship returning.

One June 27, during the early part of World War II, she was looking out the window when she saw a man coming up the long steps to the house. When she answered the bell, the man handed her a telegram, which told her that her husband's ship had been torpedoed and that all hands on board had been lost. My ghost must have been the vigilant spirit of the young widow.

THE FALLING GIRL

CARMEN M. CAMERON

The following story is sworn to be true by my dear friend from high school and her entire family:

My friend's family had lived in the same antebellum home for well over twenty years. The house was one of the few that had survived Sherman's march intact, and, along with its many other period details, the home was equipped with its own dainty and beguiling little ghost.

One day each spring the very solid-looking figure of a three-year-old girl would appear in the dark recesses of the upper hallway. She was dressed in the short hooped skirts and extravagant pantaloons typical of those once worn by the daughters of rich planters. Clutched tightly in her chubby arms she held a much worn—and apparently much beloved—rag doll. Through the years the spirit's routine never varied. After walking slowly—and rather awkwardly in her fancy clothing—down the hallway, she would stop at the landing near the top of the elegant, curved staircase to peer intently through the railing at the marble foyer below. Her attention seemed captivated by some fascinating movements—perhaps those of her parents' guests arriving yet again for the fateful soiree. In her distraction, the rag doll would slip gently from the child's loosened grasp, and in a panicked lunge, the little girl would reach too far for the cherished doll. Year after year, the child would follow the doll through the railing, "dissolving" (as did the doll) in the instant that she should have hit the black marble floor. Throughout the reenactment of this sad little drama, the child would utter not a single sound. As there was nothing terribly threatening about the ghostly visits, the family began to accept them as just another of the quaint quirks of their lovely old home.

By 1965 the visits were taken totally in stride by the entire family. That same year, the oldest daughter of the clan was invited to attend her first spring formal at the nearby college. My friend (who was eleven at the time) vividly recalls her impressions of that magical evening. As she and her mother proceeded up the stairs to fetch the primping deb, she looked back down into the entry toward where the handsome young fraternity man stood. She remembers him at that moment, slim and tall and athletic—and utterly debonair—in his black tuxedo and patent-leather shoes, a single perfect orchid enshrined in a plastic box resting on his arm. But when the three appeared on the landing a few minutes later, the young man presented an entirely different picture.

Down on one knee, the corsage box crushed, and with his hair slightly mussed, the dashing young stranger was visibly shaken. When asked what had happened, he replied, "Your little girl, ma'am, just fell from the landing. I hate to imagine what would have happened if I hadn't been here to catch her. You have to do something about that railing!" He went on, when encouraged, to explain how, in fascinated horror, he had seen the child fall. Instinctively, he had placed himself in her downward path, and the child had landed in his arms. Looking up into his eyes with a radiant smile, she had asked sweetly to be put down. Upon picking up the errant doll, she had turned with another perfect smile to say, "Thank you, sir," and, with a curtsy, had then walked calmly into the dining room and disappeared into the darkness of the room beyond.

She was never seen again.

It is improbable to assume that there is just one cause that accounts for all of the various types of apparitions that people have seen, but in this case, at least, it was a desire so all-consuming that it was strong enough to penetrate the bounds of death, time and time again. In that last bewildered moment of life, a youngster's childlike faith that she could somehow change her awful fate was charged with all the passion of a lifetime. And then, one enchanted night in spring, she found a compassionate young stranger awaiting her, and that last profound wish was finally satisfied. Perhaps the faith and innocence of a child *can* work miracles.

LOST SOULS

NIGHT SHIFT

NOREEN PFISTER

Back in 1970, I worked in the general admitting office of a small hospital deep in the brush country of Texas. I had the 11:00 p.m. to 7:00 a.m. shift, alone. One cold January night the wind outside was howling, at times pushing open the lone front door, admitting needle-sharp blasts of cold air.

That night was the first time that I was aware of "it."

I was doing paperwork, out of sight of the front door. I heard the door open, the hinges squeaking, as it made the sucking, swooshing sound so peculiar to it. Then I could hear the distinct clicking of footsteps that can be made only by a man wearing well-worn cowboy boots. There was a pause, and then a gentle rasp as the sole of a cowboy boot was drawn across the marble floor, its owner turning to speak through the grilled admitting office window.

I rose and walked to the window to greet our 2:00 a.m. visitor or patient. There was no one there. Every night thereafter the same thing happened. Sometimes I would hurry from the office to look squarely at the front door and to check to see whether someone had ducked down underneath the windowed wall, playing a trick. I questioned my co-workers, who denied any knowledge of the footsteps. I managed to scare some of them witless, and all avoided the office after midnight.

One night, at approximately 2:00 a.m., I was not in my usual place but in another part of the office, where I had a clear view of the front door. Suddenly I heard it open, the hinges squeaking slightly, the air being sucked in. As the footsteps rang out softly but distinctly, the door closed with a gentle swoosh. The steps continued—two, three, four, five, six, seven—as usual. The boot sole rasped slightly as its wearer turned.

But the door had never opened, never needed to close, and I saw no mortal make those footsteps. All irritation, curiosity, and anxiety that I had felt in prior weeks was replaced by an intense feeling of peace, protection, and friendship. I whispered softly, "Hi! I don't know who you are, but if you're lonely come on in and sit down. Stay as long as you like. I'm lonesome, too."

I never again heard this phenomenon, but I'm pleased to share with you what happened because no matter what my circumstances, I've never felt alone or lonely since. I have a friend.

Although this incident happened more than twenty years ago, as I sat down to write about it, the pen seemed to fly across the paper. I actually wondered "Am I really writing this?" I had never realized how deeply and profoundly it has changed my life.

THE GHOST WORE A SMOKING JACKET

ETHEL WILSON

We were so lucky to have found it, that roomy, airy, newly decorated flat. It had more than we had ever hoped for—plus the landlady required no lease or security deposit. My mother, my teenage siblings, and I could hardly believe our luck.

However, our landlady was a bit strange: Miss McGee was a tall, angular woman whose wispy gray hair was pulled back in an uncompromising knot, secured by old-fashioned heavy hairpins, which seemed in constant danger of falling out. She wore peculiar clothes—shapeless dresses of nondescript color and sweaters with holes in the elbow. Although her visage was grim, her manner was pleasant enough; but somehow it discouraged any kind of social exchange. She kept to herself and obviously expected us to do the same. We were instructed to put our rent in her mailbox, pick up the receipt, and ring her doorbell just once on the first day of each month.

We were too busy settling into our new home to give the reclusive Miss McGee any thought. Whenever we came in late at night, however, the two-story structure took on an eerie appearance, its old-fashioned porches and bay windows casting weird shadows. We would hurry inside and quickly turn on all of our lights. Miss McGee seemed to have an aversion to illumination. Her single light bulb, in what we presumed to be the kitchen, swung at crazy angles, casting strange shadows on her drawn shades.

Each of us kept our misgivings to ourselves until the night my brother went down to fix the furnace, which was accessible only from a communal back porch. He was so long returning that I was sent to check on him. The basement door was closed. With my heart pounding in my ears, I turned the knob, which yielded easily to my touch. My brother bolted through the door, his face ashen.

My brother, usually so cool, was visibly shaken. The door had slammed shut as he entered the basement, and the flashlight that had pierced the darkness with its bright beam abruptly went out. He had shouted, but no one had heard him, although he was sure that Miss McGee was moving about in the kitchen above him. We agreed to keep this incident to ourselves but to attend to basement chores together in the future.

The basement was not the only area that bothered us. There were sudden rushes of bone-chilling cold in rooms in which all windows and doors were closed. There was a feeling of another presence in the house whenever I entered it alone. And there was the doorbell that shrilled insistently when no one was at the door. At first we thought that neighborhood children were ringing the bell, but when the ringing persisted into the wee small hours of the morning, we were forced to admit that we did indeed have a problem, especially after the wiring checked out okay. All the while, Miss McGee glided about like a gray shadow, adding to our feelings of uneasiness. We began to leave lights on after bedtime.

There was an archway between the living room and the dining room. It was so wide that we wondered whether it had been cut oversize to accommodate a wheelchair. But if so, why were all the other doorways of normal size? We used a single lined drapery secured by a heavy tie to dress it up. We thought it was quite chic. That archway was clearly visible from my bedroom, and I always slept with my door open.

I had always been a sound sleeper, but one night I awoke from a deep sleep as though I had been rudely roused. I could see the archway clearly. The figure of a man was sharply outlined against the drapery. He was slight of build and dressed in a red smoking jacket. A white scarf with irregularly shaped polka dots was loosely knotted around his neck. In one of his hands he held a cigarette from which smoke rose in a slow, gray spiral.

Terror gripped me. I began to tremble. I opened my mouth to scream, but no sound came out. As I stared, the figure began to dissipate and the acrid smell of tobacco smoke began to fade from the air. Finally I emitted a high-pitched scream, which brought the rest of the family to my bedside. A family powwow was held as we huddled together. It was unanimous. Miss McGee accepted our notice without question. We gave no explanation.

Not until much later did we finally hear the story of the house. . . .

It had been a single-family dwelling for the McGee family, and after their parents died, Eleanor kept house for her brother, Martin. Martin developed a habit of drinking more than was good for him, and his fiancée, at her parents' urging, had broken off their engagement. Martin plunged deeper into alcoholism, despite Eleanor's efforts to help him. One night the police were summoned to the house by a hysterical Eleanor. Martin had slashed his throat, and Eleanor found him near death, slumped in the archway. He was dressed in a red smoking jacket and a smoldering cigarette lay beside him. A pool of blood was rapidly forming, spilling over onto the white scarf that was open at his neck, making round blotches.

So deep were the stains on the plaster that, when Eleanor converted the house to a two-family dwelling for economic reasons, the archway had to be cut larger to get rid of the stained plaster. After her brother's death, Eleanor lived as a recluse, seldom leaving her home, never socializing with the neighbors, and never entertaining guests. Or maybe she did, on those dark nights when doorbells shrilled in the dead of night, basement doors slammed shut, and a spectral figure in a smoking jacket roamed about, searching for the peace that obviously was denied him.

Almost fifty years later, I found myself in the area of the house. An almost overpowering urge to see the house assailed me.

What I found was a virtually vacant block. Here and there a section of fence reminded me of the orderly homes that had once stood there. Most of the lots were overgrown with weeds and stubbles of coarse grass that forced their heads above the jagged pieces of concrete, which was all that remained of the sidewalk on which I had walked so long ago. But the lot where the house had stood was barren—not a weed nor a single blade of the coarse grass broke through its dark and sullen soil. Had the weeds been cleared away? Or had they merely been unable to flourish in that unhappy ground?

I felt as though a cold, gray mist was hanging over that spot, waiting to reach out and engulf me. In spite of the summer heat I shivered, and a chill wrapped itself around me. I pushed a trembling foot down on the accelerator and sped off that street, which held for me memories of a nameless fear that was again threatening to overwhelm me! I never looked back, terrified that I might see the stark outlines of the old McGee house standing menacingly against the sky.

NAPTIME GHOST

JEANNE HALEY

One winter, more than twenty-five years ago, my husband, our four children, and I moved into the carriage house of a large, ancient estate on the shores of Lake Hopatcong, a temporary dwelling until our new home was ready. The three older children were in school; Joe, my husband, left for work at the crack of dawn; and three-year-old Larry and I were alone in the house during the day.

Larry was a charming, agreeable child, seldom causing any problems. He went in for a nap every afternoon with no complaints or fussing. Our house had the bedrooms upstairs. Larry's room was at the far end of the hall, away from the stairs.

After putting Larry in for his nap, I would go downstairs and read. One day, shortly after we had moved in, I heard noises coming from Larry's room, sounds of a small child laughing and playing.

Thinking that Larry had gotten out of bed, completely disobeying my rules, I went to his room. He was fast asleep and his toys had not been touched. This scenario was repeated often in the nine months we lived in this house. I was never able to catch Larry out of his bed; he was always sound asleep when I walked in. Larry was not the type of child to be deceitful or cleverly sneaky, and I could not imagine, at first, what was happening.

After living at Lake Hopatcong for a couple of months, I met some of my neighbors. One of them, a lovely lady in her eighties, told me many tales of the history of the lake. She had been born there and had lived there all her life. She had known Hudson Maxim, a local resident renowned for his invention of smokeless gunpowder (his brother Hiram invented the Maxim machine gun). She was a fascinating storyteller.

I didn't mention to her the strange noises in my house, for I thought that somehow they must be made by Larry, acting completely out of character. One day my neighbor told me that when she was a small girl, a family that included a three-year-old boy had lived in my house. The child had wandered away and was later found dead, drowned inside the boat house.

Immediately I knew that the sounds coming from my son's bedroom were made by this small child who had died so tragically and suddenly. I have wondered whether the next occupants of this house ever heard him playing upstairs in the nursery. Perhaps this tiny ghost craved another three-year-old playmate and found one in my son.

THE HAUNTING IN HYDE PARK

Joy Payton

It took almost two years before I gathered up the courage to talk about my encounter with anyone but my immediate family. I was sure others would think I was crazy.

In June 1979 my parents moved to Hyde Park, a neighborhood in Cincinnati, Ohio. That fall my sister Gayle and I both went off to college. When we went home for the holidays, we slept on a pullout couch in the basement. We often stayed up late, gabbing about school and watching television. Many times we felt as if someone was watching us. I attributed the strange feeling to being in an unfamiliar house, and we tried not to think about it much.

I remember that my parents often complained about lights being left on in the basement. We all insisted that we had turned them off. Gayle and I joked that our dog might be afraid of the dark and was learning new tricks.

One day the next summer I was in the living room taping music to take to college. It was just after 11:00 p.m., and I thought I might turn on the evening news. My parents were upstairs, and the house was relatively quiet. I got up from the couch and looked into the mirror over the fireplace. A man was staring back at me from the foot of the stairs in the dining room doorway.

I was horrified. Somehow a burglar must have gotten into the house, and I was alone on the first floor. I whipped around and stared right back at the stranger. He was wearing a three-piece brown tweed suit that looked as if it had been made in the 1940s. I couldn't imagine how he had gotten into the house. I hadn't heard a sound.

I could tell that the man was just as startled to see me as I was to see him. We both froze for a moment, our eyes locked, and we waited to see who would make the first move. An instant later his face softened, and he said, without speaking aloud, "Don't be afraid—I'm sorry." Then he slid sideways behind the door frame and into the dining room. I knew then that he wasn't a burglar, but I was still scared. I stayed there for several minutes. Soothing music was on the stereo, and I tried to relax.

When I regained my composure, I thought I'd better check the house to be sure that no one had broken in. I turned on all the lights, tested all the doors and windows, and finally ventured into the dining room. Everything was locked up tight. I turned off the stereo and numbly went to bed.

The next day I decided to play the music I had recorded the night before. Right at the moment the ghost had appeared, the tape became extremely distorted. An eerie, low grinding noise echoed in the background. The entire recording continued to waver and grind up to the point where I had turned off the stereo before going to bed. But the rest of that tape recorded normally.

Later I learned that often when a supernatural episode occurs, there's a change in the magnetic field. My amiable spirit had left proof of his visit by interfering with the magnetic tape.

I didn't tell my brothers about the ghost. After all, they lived in the house, and I was just visiting. But two years after this episode, my brother John told me about meeting the man in the brown tweed suit. He described the spirit exactly as I remembered him.

John was in the upstairs hall when he glanced down to see a man hovering near the base of the stairway. He looked real, except his legs stopped right below the knees. A strange light from the first floor seemed to illuminate the figure from within. My brother turned to confront the stranger. When their eyes met, the spirit slid "as if on a train track," John said. John ran into the bathroom and locked the door. He was sure that by the time he came out, the ghost would be hovering at the top of the stairs. My brother waited until morning to return to his room.

After my brother's encounter, I decided to do some research on the house. I found out that about thirty years earlier, a middle-aged man had choked to death during a holiday meal. Thankfully, I never saw the ghost again. My parents sold the house for a place in suburbia, but it was a very long time before I could look into a mirror without expecting that foreign face to be staring right back at me.

In hindsight, our ghost really seemed kind of nice. He was like a lost spirit, watching the household happenings, being a little mischievous, and, of course, scaring us. I hope by now he's found his peace.

THE ANTIQUE SHOP

LORETTA SALERNO

One day six or seven years ago, as I opened the door to my antique shop for the day, I remember feeling a little sad about being cooped up indoors. The weather had turned cold, and the air was fresh and clean. Inside was the dank, musty odor of a shop crowded with old things—furniture, pictures, and boxes of china. Lamp lights gave the place the glow of late afternoon.

There were wall sconces that could be lit, but I didn't use them anymore, not since the afternoon when my sister and I sat sipping coffee and saw them flickering—the lights growing brighter and dimmer for no apparent reason. At the same time this was happening, my sister suddenly grew pale as she stared out the front window. I turned to see what she saw but caught only a glimpse of a fleeting figure that she described as having a very old and ghostly face with hollow eyes.

There were always inexplicable happenings in the store. I've often wondered whether possessions absorb the life and feelings of their owners. Some *things* are not just inanimate objects.

I had opened the store a few years earlier and by this time had acquired a good deal of varied merchandise. It was always exciting to purchase new additions for the store, and the hunt was endless. It took me to dark basements and equally dark and mysterious attics, and almost always the items were possessions of someone deceased. They were being sold to me to be sold again. While they were in my store, they seemed to vibrate with what I called "a life of their own."

On this particular cold day, I decided to close up early. It had been a slow day, and it was getting late. Then I heard the bell on the front door ring and two people came into the shop, a man and a woman. I was quite taken aback by the sight of them. Their appearance was very strange. They wore rumpled, dirty clothes and had black soot all over them.

They seemed disoriented. The woman came closer to me, and I remember looking at her hands and arms, which were black and dirty.

Teetering on the side of her head was a hat, a bunch of old flowers pinned to it.

I was very uneasy and didn't quite know how to react, but she spoke very softly and told me what she wanted.

She said that there had been a fire in their home, and they had been moving the old furniture that had been there many years. They wanted me to look at their belongings and buy what I could use. I offered to go to their house, which was the usual policy, but they said no. They had already left the house and had their possessions in another place. I was given an address and directions and made an appointment to meet them there in an hour.

This was not a call I wanted to make alone, so my husband and I went together. All the way out I tried to describe their appearance and strangeness to him. Something just wasn't right. When we reached our destination I started looking for the house.

There were no houses.

The road I was told to travel on ended at a cemetery. We checked our directions again. We had the right place, but there were no people, no houses. Only the cemetery.

I was so confused. I couldn't figure out how I could have made a mistake. I felt upset, nervous, and fearful. We left this area and returned home.

The next morning we decided to scout out this area again. Once more, we arrived at the gates of the cemetery. I returned to work to make inquiries. It turned out that there had been a fire about a week before in a house not far from my shop.

When I went to see the house, I was sick from head to toe. Most of it was gone, the rest boarded up. It had been a disastrous fire. The neighbor told me that two people were killed in the house, a man and a woman. Same age, same description as my callers.

THE SOBBING WOMAN

CHARLES ROGERS

My grandmother made it her business to buy houses that had seen better days. She and my father would patch them up and resell them for a small profit. So when I was a youngster I spent a lot of time around some strange places. I remember abandoned houses with tattered curtains waving like skeletal fingers through broken windows and farmhouses that looked as though the land they sat on was reclaiming them a day at a time. But the house I will never forget was the one in a small town in northwestern Pennsylvania.

The home was set back from the quiet road that passed before it. A backyard tolerated a crumbling walkway of red brick that was being pushed up by the grass beneath it. The previous owner had planted a small flower garden. It was thickly overgrown.

I was fourteen years old and my job on this summer day was to clean the basement. After an hour or two I wandered out to the backyard to sit in the shade. While resting there I glanced upward to a window overlooking the garden. I was startled to see a woman sitting by the window. Who was she? As far as I knew only my grandmother and father were in the house. Then I thought, perhaps she was someone they knew and was visiting. She did not seem to be looking at any one thing but held her gaze steadily toward the back of the yard. If she noticed me I could not tell. I felt as though I was intruding and did not attempt to catch her eye. I suppose there was nothing remarkable about her features since I cannot recall anything in particular.

I was a little frightened and wanted to leave, but I also didn't want her to see me so I stayed where I was. What really scared me was what happened next. She raised her arms slowly and placed a white cloth over her head so that her face was completely covered. It was time to get out of there. When I stood up I could hear her sobbing under the cloth. I didn't look anymore but ran to the front of the house.

I found my grandmother on the porch and told her what I had seen. I hoped for an explanation but instead she said nothing and turned and went into the house. We passed my father, who was working on the stairway, and my grandmother told him about the lady upstairs. "There was no way anyone could have gotten upstairs without my seeing them," my father said. He had been there all morning.

My grandmother ushered us up to the room overlooking the garden. It was empty. There was nothing extraordinary—just an old-fashioned bedroom long unused. My father opened the door to the closet. He peered into the poor light and pulled out a folded wheelchair.

There was no fuss made about this event, and I never heard much about it after that day. We went on with our work, although I tried to avoid going upstairs as much as I could, and I never looked up at that window again. The house was sold and that was the end of it. But I overheard a conversation a few years later in which my grandmother made known her true thoughts on my sighting.

She had found out that the house had been the scene of a brutal murder.

Sometime in the early forties a man had killed his wife there. In a drunken rage he beat her with his fists and then pushed the poor woman down the stairway. She was helpless because she had been confined to a wheelchair. He fled and it was a week before her body was found.

I had seen a ghost. What else could it have been?

DARK INTRUDER

JENNIFER MATERA

In the midst of dark, overhanging trees stood my family's old house. Strange things happened while I was living there, and these experiences shaped my beliefs about the existence of ghosts.

It was on a cold wintry night that I first encountered the unwanted visitor in our house. I remember lying in my mother's bed because it was warmer in her room, and both my parents and sister were out for the evening. I was alone with just my thoughts to keep me company. I had nearly fallen asleep when I heard the sound of footsteps in the hall. I immediately saw the figure of a tall, dark man, luminous in appearance, in the doorway. His clothes were black, and he wore a brimmed hat on his head. I could vaguely make out a cape, which hung loosely around his shoulders.

Numbed with fear, I stared at the advancing figure. "Oh, please don't come any closer!" I thought to myself. My attention was drawn hypnotically to his eyes, which had the somber look of a man who delighted in evil destruction. I hastily looked for a weapon to use against him. An old pair of shoes was nearby that would serve my purpose. I reached over and grabbed them and flung them right at him. He vanished into thin air. Sanity reestablished itself in my mind. I felt safe again—until the next time he appeared.

Sometime later my sister began complaining of disturbing nightmares. One night I agreed to keep her company at bedtime. We retired late that evening, and I lay down on the extra bed in her room. I was listening for the train that passed by at the same time each night. I sat up to see whether I could catch a glimpse of it as it roared by. Instead I saw him again, this time sitting on a chair by the bedroom window. His hand rested underneath his chin as if he were in deep thought, his face turned away from me. I wondered to myself whether he was also waiting for the train to pass by. Would he be able to hear it?

I was curious about what he was thinking, but I was careful not to disturb him. But then, with a perfectly involuntary movement, I leaned toward him. My curiosity had engulfed my better sense of judgment. As I moved, he suddenly jerked his head around toward me, and for just a moment I looked into a face that looked like that of a corpse. Impulsively, I turned away with disgust. When I looked back, he was gone.

The third encounter was of a more violent nature. It was during the summer, and we all liked to keep our windows open to get the cool breezes that came up at night. My parents and I were awakened from sleep that night by bloodcurdling screams. We all rose quickly from our beds and ran down the hallway to where the screams were coming from—my sister's room. We opened her bedroom door and found her clutching her throat. After we calmed her, she began to tell us what had happened. "A tall man," she said, "with dark eyes and old-fashioned clothes was trying to strangle me!" Her screams, she felt, had scared him away. She had always been very levelheaded with not much of an imagination. Now terror filled her eyes, and her description of her assailant was enough for me to realize that she was describing the man I'd seen.

Perhaps thinking that we had been tormented enough, I set out to discover why all of this was happening. After lengthy research into old newspaper articles and public records, I found the answer. Old real-estate records showed that the house had been constructed in the late 1800s and that people had rented rooms there by the week or month. Most didn't stay very long. The house was sold to my parents in the early 1940s, and they later made it into a one-family home. After several late evenings at the library, I also came across an old newspaper article that revealed a significant fact. Printed in a column relating local news was the story of a man who had committed suicide in his room in a boardinghouse. It didn't give much detail, only his name and address. It didn't surprise me to see that the address was the same as that of our house.

I discontinued research after that. I guess I just didn't want to know any more about him. I moved out of my parents' home shortly thereafter. I know he is still there.

A LONELY CHILD

CARLA S. MAZURIK

We have a little ghost living with us. I became aware of her presence shortly after moving into our farm, which was deeded in 1878. While I was cleaning out the cellar of the guest house, I saw something block out the light as it passed by the grime-covered window. I assumed it was one of my kids, so I started talking to "it." Getting no response, I looked out the door and saw my daughter quite a distance away. There was no one else in sight. My daughter said she had not been near that window.

As time went on, we would often catch a glimpse of a white wisp peeking around the barn and disappearing; sometimes it would look around from the side of the house. Since it stood as tall as the bottom of the electric meter on the house, we assumed it to be a child.

After telling our "ghost story" to several people, I learned that there had been a house nearby years and years ago. In it had lived a little girl who had pulled a kerosene lamp over onto herself and had burned to death. Could she be our ghost?

Late at night we could hear music playing somewhere in the house, just loud enough to be distinguished as music but never loud enough for us to identify the type of music. One time my children left a radio playing loudly upstairs, and after I had had quite enough of that noise, I yelled upstairs for them to turn it off. The music promptly stopped, and a few minutes later my son walked into the house. Again, my daughter was not close by; she too had been outside. I checked the radio, and the switch had been turned off.

Around Christmastime one year, we had a glass crash to the kitchen floor from the counter for no apparent reason. Thinking that perhaps our ghost was upset about not getting a Christmas present, I bought a small teddy bear for her. For a period of time after that, the bear was frequently moved, as if it had been played with. Since then, I have bought her a gift every Christmas, but she does not seem to touch them.

Her presence is now becoming less and less frequent; once in a great while we'll still see the white shadow in a room, as if she has come back to say hello.

I often have wondered: Was she drawn here during the time my children were small, but moved on now that they are grown?

A SEDONA GHOST

CAROL ST. JOHN

My new job at a vegetarian restaurant in Sedona, Arizona, included living quarters downstairs. Another woman and I occupied two rooms in which the restaurant manager had previously lived. "The place is haunted," he said. "I would hear the chairs sliding across the wood floor in the restaurant, and when I went up to see whether someone had gotten in, there was never anyone there."

One evening when the place was closed and dark, my friend came to my door. "Did you hear that?" she asked, wide-eyed. Yes, I had. "Do you think somebody is up there?" I doubted it. It wasn't the only night we had heard the chairs.

But that was just the beginning. After the restaurant went out of business, the manager didn't want the building empty, so another friend and I occupied the downstairs rooms. The place was big and vacant and dark, and whenever I entered it, it seemed creepy—evil-in-the-dark creepy. Even in the daytime. Something was always whispering frightening ideas over my shoulder and into my mind.

I had read about this stuff—it must be a ghost. I knew that I had the spiritual right to order evil out of my space, and I called for angelic protection. I knew the ghost couldn't hurt me, but I sure could feel that it was there. My room stayed very cozy because my angel was on the job. I went upstairs only in daylight.

The building was on a slope, with the front of the restaurant on street level upstairs and our downstairs rooms at ground level in the back. I was sitting in the backyard one day and looked up at the big picture window of the restaurant. I saw something there. But I can't say I saw it physically. It was like seeing something in a dream, but I was awake, and the sun was out. The window was filled with something that had black eyes and writhing tentacles. It made a sound I couldn't really hear—"Aaaaahh!" It leered at me, squirming. Amazed, I studied the window. There were no drapes, and the room behind the window was dark. It reminded me of a childhood image from a comic book, the night forest filled with eyes called one-eyed wobblies. I asked my friend, "Do you see anything strange about that window?"

"Oooh," she said. "Eyes, tentacles—it's weird!"

Finally, we rented the whole building, and it became a lively cooperative restaurant and living quarters. Sedona is a tourist town; lots of people come through. Residents came to know the ghost. His scraping chairs were heard often; his creepy vibes were felt in empty spaces; his striking appearance at the window was even seen by a few.

Don't get me wrong—we didn't talk about this to everyone because we didn't want to scare customers away. But every now and then some perceptive person would say, "Do you think this place could be haunted?" or "There's a weird feeling in here." Then we would say "Oh, that's Arthur, our resident ghost." We had even named him.

Under one staircase there was a small unfinished closet with a dirt floor. We had cleaned some trash out of it, but it wasn't fit to hold anything good. We declared it Arthur's room and banished him to it. (We had tried to exorcise him but it didn't work.) So we kept Arthur in the closet. His creepiness could no longer be felt anywhere, unless you opened his door. The chairs kept quiet.

Some people we knew had their own idea about the place: long ago a robber had stolen some money—either gold or silver—and had buried it on the property. He'd been caught and lynched right there. Was Arthur this robber, trying to protect his loot? A few folks felt this so strongly that they tried metal detectors and dowsing psychometry in search of the buried treasure. A few holes were dug. Nothing came of it.

A few years later the place sat vacant for a while and then was torn down. I never heard from Arthur again.

NOISES IN THE NIGHT

CORA R. KAEMPFER

By 1945 World War II had ended, and, like many veterans and their families, my husband and I joined the trek west to California, though we did not have family out there and had no housing arranged. As soon as we arrived, I discovered that I was pregnant. Sacramento was so crowded that hotels had a three-day limit on how long guests could stay. We turned to the chamber of commerce for help.

The young woman whose city brochures had helped entice us to the capital of California was sympathetic, and she sent us to share an upper flat with another couple, Alma and George, who were between houses. We found them compatible, and they "adopted" us, treating us as impulsive children. They had the front half of the flat—one bedroom and the living room; we had the dining room, one bedroom, and the kitchen; we shared the bathroom. The house was on N Street, next to the California Fruit Exchange building, in what was once a distinguished older neighborhood.

The first night we lay awake for a while, congratulating ourselves on the good fortune of having a roof over our heads and a warm bed. Then we fell asleep in exhaustion and relief.

The next night was not the same. We had spent a congenial evening visiting with Alma and George, hearing about their daughters, and when we got ready for bed we were thankful for the good companions we had found. But later that night we were both awakened by footsteps in our hallway. At first we thought that our friends were walking near the bathroom, but the steps went beyond the bathroom, and they sounded strange. We wondered whether someone had pried open the door and had come up the staircase from the common front door.

My husband went out to investigate, and I followed. The front door was locked, our companions seemed asleep, and we were puzzled. We checked the back door, too, and found it securely locked. There was no way a man could have entered through a second-story window. We went back to bed, relieved but still puzzled.

We discussed having dreamed it, but could both of us have had the same dream? And then one night we heard them again, the footsteps in the hallway, going past our bedroom. But no one had passed our door. We turned on the hall light to watch; we still heard the footsteps, but no one appeared. We decided not to embarrass ourselves by mentioning it to our neighbors. But the next night the same thing occurred, and we were getting no rest. After the third night, we decided to tell Alma and George.

After I finished my story, and after we had observed them giving one another worried looks, Alma said, "Don't worry about it, Cora, but after you've had the baby, I'll explain." Naturally, I thought it had something to do with them, and I refrained from any further questioning, though I was not able to figure out why my having a baby would make a difference. The noises continued, and we continued checking, but after a few weeks we started sleeping without paying attention—we were exhausted, and whatever it was seemed benign.

Months later, after we had bought our own home and were enjoying our new baby, Alma and George were our guests at dinner. Of course, I now asked for the promised explanation.

Alma hesitated, and then said, "Well, I think you can handle it now. But I didn't know you well enough then to tell you the story. It took *us* awhile to come to terms with it. But there was no place else to move to. So we decided to live with our ghosts.

"You see, a former occupant had committed suicide in the bathroom. He cut his throat. I didn't think this was a story for an expectant mother. And then the husband of the owner of the house died in what was your dining room. There were rumors that he was done in—but this was never proved. So when you told me of hearing footsteps, but never seeing anyone, well, it wasn't that hard for us to assume that you were aware of some ghosts coming back to their old haunts."

I was glad Alma had been discreet. Even though the ghosts intended no harm to us, I was happy I hadn't heard their stories while we lived there. A few years after we moved away, the old house was torn down and a multistory garage now stands in its place. I wonder where the ghosts are now.

A DISTINCT ODOR OF BLOOD

J. DAVID MOELLER

I'm a struggling actor, and in the winter of 1981 I had just moved back to Dallas from New York City. I'd been cast in a theatrical production of Marsha Norman's prizewinning play *Getting Out*. As is usual for many actors, I was low on funds and needed an apartment close to the theater at a price I could afford, so I answered an ad for one located just around the corner.

When the landlady showed it to me, the first thing I noticed was the distinct odor of blood as I walked over the threshold. She remained in the hall.

"Do you mind if I glance around a little bit?" I asked her, wondering why she was just standing there.

"Of course, take all the time you need," she said before making a beeline for her office.

It was a simple two-room flat, heated by a gas wall heater in the living room. I stepped over to test it, and about two feet away from it I again noticed an odor of blood. I hadn't really paid attention to it before because it had passed so quickly, but this time I was standing still, and the sensation was very real. I looked, but there were no stains on the apparently new carpet. The smell disappeared when I moved on.

In all other respects the place was just what I wanted, so I took it.

My first night there was distressing—I couldn't fall asleep. Something was keeping me awake. After much tossing and turning I decided to put my bed in another position in the room. I almost drifted off, and then I was awakened with a start. I tried another position, but still sleep eluded me. Four times I moved the bed and four times I was suddenly awakened for no apparent reason. All the time this was going on I kept glancing around the room to see whether there was something about the place I was missing. I could see nothing out of the ordinary.

Because the temperatures in Dallas that winter were unusually cold, I finally decided to move into the living room where it was warmer. As I passed the heater I picked up the odor of blood again. What had happened here? Bloody murder? And why were there only two places—the entrance and near the heater—where I could smell the blood?

Thinking back on her actions, I concluded that my landlady knew something—but she wasn't about to tell a new renter that his apartment might be haunted!

Could it be? Noooo. There are no such things as ghosts. And with that thought I fell asleep.

A few weeks later, after a cast party, I was settled in for a good sleep. The heater was on low, I could hear a brisk wind outside, and there was talk of snow before dawn. I remember drifting off thinking about the snow. Suddenly I was wide awake! I was facing the wall, but I knew I was not alone. Someone, or something, was behind me there in the room.

Every hair on my body stood on end. I was staring at the blank wall, listening for any movement: the rustle of feet on carpet, the brush of cloth against a door frame, the inhalation of air whistling through nostrils. Anything that would give me the slightest clue as to who was there watching me.

After what seemed like several minutes, but in reality was maybe only one, I slowly began to turn over. I didn't want to alert my visitor. I didn't want to appear threatening in any way. Somehow I knew instinctively that whoever or whatever was there was not a threat to me. I turned my head to the side so I could see the whole room.

And there it was: a ghost!

I think it was a she-ghost, a child. She was about three feet tall and was more like an oblong shape of smoke than a formed body, but somehow it "seemed" like a body. And she was looking right at me! She had no head, but the top of the form, although eyeless, was very obviously aware of me and was looking in my direction.

Naturally, I thought this was a trick of my sleepy eyes. I had had nothing to drink, and I don't smoke—so it wasn't a cigarette I'd left burning. I fixed my eyes on her and moved my head from side to side to see whether it was what they call floaters in my eyes. Then I focused my eyes about three feet to her right and, with my peripheral vision, could see she was still there—about two feet in front of the heater.

I turned on my side toward her and looked. She looked back. Understand, these looks were sensations, but they were just as real as if someone human and alive had been in the room with me. She didn't move around; she undulated in place. I could see through her, as if I were looking through cloudy glass.

Believe it or not, without either of us uttering a sound, there was communication between us. Not sentences, but feelings. Emotions. She was lonely. And she was curious about me. She was a little afraid, and I let her know, by thinking and actually feeling it, that there was nothing to be afraid of and that everything was all right now.

And then I rolled back over on my side and started to go to sleep again, like a parent reassuring a child with his voice in the night and going back to sleep.

A few minutes later I was wide-eyed again. I was still facing the wall, but now I was also facing my visitor: she had moved. She was standing about a foot in front of me, looking down at me. I looked up at her and wondered why she was still there. Immediately I got my answer. A feeling of serenity came over me—she had come to thank me and to say good-bye.

That night I slept like a baby.

The next morning I asked my landlady about the apartment. I told her I'd had trouble sleeping the first night and asked whether anyone had died in the place. She gave me a look of horror, wondering how I knew to ask that, and answered only that an old woman had had a heart attack in the bedroom shortly before I'd moved in. (I wondered whether she'd seen my little friend and been frightened to death.)

Then I asked her about the smell of blood, and she dismissed me quickly with the statement that she didn't know what I was talking about and refused to discuss it any further.

When I went back into my place I couldn't help noticing how fresh and clean the place smelled—all over. And I smiled to myself.

THE ATTIC STAIRS

MICKEY CRIST

My mother grew up in the middle of the Great Depression in a large, old creaky house in Colorado Springs. After her family moved into this house, they were informed by the neighbors that a previous resident had hanged himself in the attic and that the house was haunted. This frightened the three kids considerably and, as a consequence, nobody in the family went near the third floor stairway, which led to the door of the attic. The door was locked, and, as far as anyone was concerned, it could stay that way.

One day a year or so after the family had moved into the old house, my mother noticed that there was a set of footprints in the dust of the stairway leading up to the door of the attic. She immediately went running to my grandmother and told her what she had seen. My grandmother could not imagine whose footsteps they were, because she had strictly forbidden the kids to go near the attic door.

She went out into the yard and got my grandfather. He crept up to the third floor and stared at the flight of stairs leading up to the attic door. My grandfather was a part-time sheriff's officer and was trained to notice details. He saw that the footprints in the dust leading up the stairway to the door went up but did not come back down. He immediately assumed that a vagrant had somehow gotten into the house and had decided to take up residence in the attic.

He crept up the stairs, pistol and flashlight in hand, and slowly unlocked the door. He shined his flashlight into the attic and then went in. He immediately noticed that not only was the attic as empty as it had been the day they had moved in but that there were no footprints of any kind in the dust on the attic floor. And there was only one way into and out of the attic.

My grandfather could not explain the presence of the footprints in the dust. The only logical explanation that could be made was that the ghost of the previous resident was prowling the halls of the third floor of the old house and had finally worked up enough nerve to return to the attic where he, in life, had committed suicide.

GHOST HUNT

SARA WILSON

I have always been interested in parapsychology and the supernatural and have taken some classes relating to these subjects. When I heard about a "haunted house" for sale several miles down the road, I was fascinated.

The house was listed with a Realtor, and because I lived in the area I felt I had to justify why I wanted to look at it. I finally concocted a story about my mother hoping to move near me and said that we were looking for a small house to purchase for her. I made an appointment to go see the house and dragged my husband along, too.

It was a hot summer night in August, without a breath of wind. The Realtor was there when we arrived. When she unlocked the door, there was such a cold blast of air that I couldn't believe it.

The house had been vacant for some time, and I could understand why. On the walls of one of the bedrooms were pasted hundreds of shards of glass, all sizes and shapes. It looked as if they had come from a broken mirror. Covering the walls of the other rooms were cutouts of the moon, sun, and stars in different formations. In all of the rooms, even in the bedrooms, there were beautiful chandeliers made of crystal. Although they were dusty and dirty, they were obviously beautiful. I asked the Realtor about the bizarre decorations, and she said rumor had it that Gypsies had lived there and that one had been murdered there.

We then said our good-byes and, after the Realtor left, returned to the house. It was almost dusk at that time and, although we could not get into the house, we walked into the backyard. There was a small fountain there, with benches on either side, and several trees and bushes overhanging it. I sat down on one of the benches while my husband walked around. Suddenly I felt a cold blast of air pass over me. I started to talk, as though there was someone there, saying, "I would like to help you if you let me. Is there anything I can do?" I talked quietly for several minutes and was very intent on what I was doing. Suddenly I heard my husband whisper, "Look at that!" When I raised my eyes, I saw a small whirlwind kicking up the dirt under one of the trees. Bear in mind that up until that moment there had been no breeze at all. I kept on talking, saying things like "I care about you. How can I help? Are you lost? You can leave if you want to, but you are safe here."

Slowly the whirlwind moved up into the air and around my head several times. I could feel the strong breeze it created; my hair was blowing out from my head as though I were in the middle of a windstorm. Then it moved away into a tree and stopped. Not a leaf rustled or moved anywhere. My heart was pounding, and my husband was ready to drag me out of there.

I sat very still and then got up and walked around the area for a few minutes. It was getting dark quickly by then, and I began to be uneasy. But I wanted to try it one more time, so I sat down again and began to say the same things as before. I also said "It's okay if you want to go now. There is no reason for you to stay. You can be happy." As I was talking, the whirlwind suddenly came out of another tree and stopped right over my head. It hovered there for a moment and then began to descend. I sat very still; suddenly I experienced what felt like a million little feathers softly touching my face. It was almost like gentle little kisses. Just as quickly as it began, it stopped, and the whirlwind moved straight up from my head and disappeared. It was as though it had never been there. Needless to say, we hastily left the yard. When we got home, my husband said, "If I hadn't been there to see that, I would never have believed it!"

Soon after, the For Sale sign was taken down and a family moved in. I guess the spirit found its way back. I hope I helped.

ALONE IN THE HOUSE

BONNIE SMITH

When I was thirteen years old and my brother was eleven, our family moved to a small town in North Carolina. We were able to rent a huge old house next door to a church.

From the very first day, strange things happened. We would hear someone calling us by name from elsewhere in the house and, upon investigating, would find that either nobody in the family had called us or that no one else was home.

It was not uncommon for any of us to be followed from room to room when we were alone in the house. "Something" whistled softly in our ear as if someone were hanging over our shoulder. We were awakened almost nightly by loud footsteps in the attic, and we would find the attic door wide open in the morning. Articles that we set down in one room would suddenly disappear, only to be found in the basement or on the back porch. Most of the things that happened could be explained away as forgetfulness or overactive imaginations, yet two specific incidents convinced my brother, my mother, and me that there truly was a ghost in our house.

The first incident occurred on Christmas Eve while our parents were attending a company party. My brother and I were left with the family dog for a couple of hours. We were sitting in the living room watching television when loud banging sounds came from the upstairs hallway. Then the stairway banister shook with such force that I was sure it would break into pieces at any moment. The dog barked and howled.

Dressed only in slippers and pajamas, we hesitated to run out into the snow. But, sure that our lives were in danger, we dived into the tiny bathroom beneath the stairway—it was the only room equipped with a door latch. We sat on the floor together with our backs pressed against the wall and our feet firmly planted against the door. We held the dog as she whined.

Within moments, heavy footsteps sounded on the stairs over our heads. They stopped at the bottom of the stairs. We heard no sounds other than our own breathing for many minutes. Suddenly we heard the front door open and felt cold air rush under the bathroom door. Just as suddenly, the front door slammed shut. There was silence for what seemed like hours, yet we were still afraid to leave our hiding place. We heard the front door open and close again, but we did not emerge until we heard our mother's voice call to us.

After we told our story, our dad checked the house but found no way for anyone to have entered in their absence.

The second incident occurred several months later. My brother and I arrived home from school to an empty house. There was music blasting so loud that we had to shout at each other to be heard. We followed the music upstairs to his bedroom. My brother's only radio was unplugged and in pieces in a box under his bed (he had taken it apart to see how it worked). Once we had built up the courage, we walked over to his bed and pulled the box out into view. The music stopped immediately! The two of us ran out of the house and sat on the curb until our parents came home from work.

As children will do, we adjusted to the everyday antics of our live-in ghost. We named him Oscar and began to tell our new friends at school about him. It was then that we found out that we lived in a well-known "haunted house" and that was why so few of our friends were permitted to come to our home. We were told the story of why people never lived in the house more than a short time.

Many years ago the church-owned house was a rectory inhabited by the minister and his family. He and his seventeen-year-old son did not get along and frequently fought. The boy would usually take refuge in the huge attic. One day in the midst of a heated argument, the minister chased his son from the attic. They both made it safely down the steep attic stairs, but the boy tripped and fell down the stairs leading to the first floor. When he hit the wall at the bottom, he broke his neck and died. The minister and his remaining family were driven out of the house soon afterward by a ghost. Supposedly, the house had been haunted since then.

We lived in that house for nine months, and then we returned to Michigan.

Some twenty years later, my parents revisited that small town in North Carolina. The haunted house is gone now with only the chimney still standing. I only hope that poor Oscar has finally found peace.

THE DOLLHOUSE VISITOR

PAT MIGHELL PAXTON

We had lived in our newly constructed home only four months when Ming, our Siamese cat, and I came upon an adorable little translucent girl playing with a dollhouse in our four-year-old daughter's room.

Our home is a two-story Colonial furnished with primitive antiques and reproductions and is situated two-hundred yards from the white frame house that was the center of the farm that became our subdivision in the 1960s. Because both houses are nestled atop a knoll on an otherwise flat stretch of prairie, it is conceivable that our home is situated on the site of a settler's cabin or a smaller, less pretentious prairie home than the present rambling farmhouse. The handwrought nails that have emerged in our lawn and garden after a rain attest to some sort of early structure on the site and could also account for our little visitor.

Ming and I were the only two family members in the house that crisp and sunny October morning. My husband was at his office, our two sons in school, and Jodi was half a block away playing with a friend. The sheets from four beds had dried quickly on the clothesline, and by 11:00 a.m. I was putting them back on the beds, a task Ming always enjoyed helping me accomplish. I had taken a few minutes to play with him in the master bedroom, and with his feline imagination running wild, he raced from the room ahead of me. The autumn sun, slanting through the easterly window in Jodi's room, gave a golden glow to the hall.

Jodi's dollhouse had been mine as a child, and she was already finding as much enjoyment in it as I had years before. She could spend hours arranging the furniture or making up family dramas to be carried out by the dollhouse people. While most of the children's toys were put away when not in use, some toys were played with over a period of days or weeks and then relegated to a shelf or a closet. So Jodi had left her dollhouse on a braided rug in the center of her room where it awaited her return and resumption of play after lunch.

I was just outside Jodi's bedroom door when I first saw "her." The sight of a strange child in my daughter's room caught me totally off guard. She was in a squatting position, playing with the dollhouse! What transpired took only seconds, much less time than it will take to describe.

The child was small-boned and exactly Jodi's size—small for four years of age. She had waist-long thick brown hair tied with a ribbon at the top. She had a beautiful little face with wide dark eyes that gazed straight into mine when she turned to look at me. She was wearing black high-top shoes, black stockings, and a below-the-knee, dark brown dress with long sleeves and petticoats beneath the skirt. There were several small darts in the fitted bodice, a neatly tied bow at the skirt back, and delicate lace edging at the neck and wrists. Her back was toward me but she turned twice to look at me, displaying the universal expression found on the face of a child caught doing something considered off limits. While observing all these details I was very aware that I was looking right through her!

I stood clutching the top railing of the open staircase outside the door, staring in total disbelief at this diminutive stranger dressed in nineteenth-century clothing. I must have frightened her with my staring, because she suddenly arose, kicked up her heels, and made a hasty departure across the room and right out through the wall beneath the window.

It took several seconds for me to fully comprehend what had just occurred, and it was then that I became conscious of Ming. He was beside me, and every hair on his usually sleek body was standing straight out. He slowly made his way into Jodi's room, cautiously approaching the dollhouse. I watched his nostrils dilate with each sniff of the air; then, still resembling a porcupine, he ran from the room, going clear downstairs to regain his cool-cat composure.

The little girl came to play twenty-six years ago and to my knowledge has never returned. There was certainly nothing frightening about her, it was not a dark night with thunder and lightning, and she was in a brand-new house—all things not usually associated with a ghost sighting. And to top it off, she was doing something I have not heard of a ghost doing: she was playing.

Jodi is now a beautiful woman, I am the grandmother of four boys, Ming is in kitty heaven, and the dollhouse sits upstairs in a quiet playroom awaiting that special touch from yet another generation of little girl—a living, breathing, real little girl!

HELP FROM BEYOND

MAMA

REBA KIRKENDALL

I never believed in supernatural encounters until I had one myself. It occurred in March 1959.

Construction work was scarce, and since there were no jobs to be found locally, Dean, my husband, had gone with three other pipe fitters to Michigan to work. We were living in a big two-story house that we were renting. Our boys were nine and ten years old, we had a daughter who was six, and our baby girl was three months. The run-down house was old, but it was all we could afford at the time. The second floor was just one big room. Since we didn't use it, I had stretched a clothesline across it, and when the weather was bad I hung the laundry up there to dry. The steep, winding staircase leading to the upstairs room cast long, dark, eerie shadows on the wall during the evening. The house creaked and groaned at night, and I was more than a little afraid without Dean there.

There was a nice house two doors down the street that had been for rent for a while. When my brother-in-law stopped by one day for a cup of coffee, I told him about the house and said I wished I had it. I was sure, though, that I couldn't afford it.

My brother-in-law came back later that day and told me that he had talked to the man who owned the house and found out it was renting for only ten dollars more a month than we were paying. He offered to move our furniture in his truck.

I rented the house that day and in two days we were completely moved. The new house was so much nicer and warmer than the old one, and the kids enjoyed having a larger yard to play in.

The third night we were there I was still unpacking. Since I had only a couple of boxes more to go, I decided to finish before I went to bed. I fixed supper for the kids and myself, and after their baths and getting them all settled down for the night I went about emptying the last two boxes. By the time I finished I was tired, so I decided to leave the dishes until morning. I went to bed and slept a peaceful sleep. I wasn't afraid here.

The next morning I awoke when the baby cried to let me know she was hungry. I changed her and went into the kitchen to warm a bottle. As the milk heated, I put a pot of coffee on to perk. Testing the bottle on my wrist, I went in to feed the baby.

As I sat in the rocker feeding her, it suddenly dawned on me that something was different. I couldn't figure out what it was. When the baby was through eating I laid her down in her crib and went in to get a cup of coffee. As I reached for a cup, I stopped. The dishes that had been stacked on the counter the night before were now clean and in the cupboard. The counter had been wiped clean. I turned toward the table. The chairs were pushed up on each side of it and it was clean, too. I sat down and took a sip of coffee. Had I washed the dishes and forgotten it? No, I knew I hadn't. I checked the back door to see whether it was locked. It was. I went to the front door and saw that the night latch was still secure. I couldn't understand it.

I fixed breakfast and woke the kids. As they ate I asked the boys, "Did you two wash the dishes last night?" They looked at each other and Mike said, "No. Were we supposed to? You didn't tell us." "No, no," I said, "that's all right."

I pushed the incident out of my mind. I was so busy the next two days getting settled, I didn't have time to dwell on it. I decided I had, after all, washed the dishes, and, because I was so tired, had forgotten. Dean was coming home for the weekend, and I wanted to have everything all nice and straightened up and put away so I could show off our new home. I wasn't sure how he was going to react to my moving without letting him know, but I felt pretty sure he would be as glad as I was to get out of the drafty old house and into this nice, comfortable home.

I was right. After dinner was over and the kids had told him about moving and what they had done all week, we got settled down for the night. We talked a while and went to bed.

During the night the weather started turning cold and the blowing wind woke me. I got up and put another blanket on the bed and went into the boys' room to check on them. They were sleeping soundly and seemed to be warm enough. I went to look in on Kathy, the six-year-old. I decided she might need some more covers.

As I went out into the hall to the linen closet, I saw her. Even today I don't know why I knew immediately it was a woman. A white figure floated softly in front of me down the hall and turned into the kitchen. I wasn't afraid, only curious. I followed her into the kitchen and turned the light on. Everything was as I had left it before going to bed, and the figure had disappeared. I went back to bed.

I lay there in the dark and thought about what I had seen. Should I wake Dean up and tell him? He would just tell me I had been dreaming. I hadn't told him about the dishes being washed right after I had moved; I knew he would just tease me and tell me that I was imagining things. And why wasn't I scared? I had been afraid in the old two-story house, and nothing like this had ever happened.

Dean returned to Michigan on Monday to go back to work. Late that afternoon my sister came by to see me, and while she was there my brother stopped in. We were sitting in the kitchen having coffee and talking when my sister touched my arm and pointed to the door. The knob was turning. I whispered to my brother; he slipped out the front door and went around the house. The back door opened out into a small screened-in porch. My brother came back in the front door and into the kitchen. He said, "The screen door is locked and the porch is empty."

As we watched, the doorknob turned again. My brother walked over and unlocked the door. There was nothing on the porch, and the screen was latched from the inside. He said, "Well, no one is here." I told them about the strange things that had happened and about seeing the figure in the hall. I said, "I guess I had her locked out and she wanted in." My brother laughed and said, "Oh, it was just the wind or something," and

I knew that he and my sister thought I had imagined the things I told them.

I saw the white floating figure several more times. Once in the daytime, as I walked down the hall to the bathroom, I felt a soft cool breeze touch my face, and I saw a large object that was wispy, like a white spiderweb. As it passed quietly by me, it took the form of a woman—an old woman—with soft, brown hair done up in a knot on top of her head. For a second I looked into the kindest, warmest eyes I had ever seen. She smiled. Then she was gone.

The first of the month I went to pay the rent. The man who owned the house also owned a 5-and-10-cent store a few blocks away. I went into his office, and as I wrote a check for the rent I said, "Did you know your house is haunted?" I expected him to laugh or something. But he said, "Is Mama bothering you?" I looked at him and he said, "That is my old home. I was born there and I would like to live in it, but my wife says Mama is still there and it bothers her." I said, "Well, at last someone believes me," and I told him about the things that had happened. He said that he had had people move out because of the strange happenings.

Then my landlord asked, "Are you afraid to live there?" I said, "Oh, no! I love it, and I look forward to the times I see her. I have the feeling that she likes me and my children." He took my check and tore it in two. He said, "This is just between me and you. You can live there as long as you want. There will be no more rent. Just be good to Mama."

Each month I took the money I would have paid for rent and saved it. We lived in Mama's house for sixteen months. After that I never mentioned to anyone the times I'd find the dishes done in the morning or the laundry folded or the nights when I walked into the children's rooms and saw them being tucked in tenderly by a soft, white figure as they slept.

I would have bought the house, but the owner didn't want to sell. So I took my savings and made a down payment on the house we live in now. Sometimes I drive by "Mama's house" and wonder—is she still there? Once I talked to the landlord, and he said he had rented the house to several different families since we left. No one had ever mentioned seeing anything strange.

If Dean ever wondered how I saved enough money from my rent and household money for a down payment on our home, he didn't mention it. I guess he thought I was just a good manager. I let him think so. Besides, the landlord is dead now so I couldn't prove that he let me have the house rent-free. If I had told Dean, I doubt that he would have believed me about the rent or anything else that happened. I wouldn't blame him. You have to have it happen to you before you truly believe.

MY GUARDIAN ANGEL

JUDY WALTERS

Do you believe in guardian angels or good ghosts? I never did until 1977 when one guided me away from certain injury or even death.

The incident occurred when I was living in California. I had been taking care of my mother-in-law, who was very sick. It was right before Christmas, so I decided to go shopping one day. I asked my mother-in-law, "What can I get you for Christmas?" She answered, "I'd like a picture of Christ." So I left for my shopping tour.

I couldn't go too far from home, as I might be needed there. Not far away, in the downtown area, was a store that carried religious books and objects, so I went there and found a picture I thought my mother-in-law would like. I asked the clerk to wrap it as a gift. When I left the store I walked to the corner of a busy intersection and pressed the signal for the pedestrian walk sign. As it flashed on, I stepped off the curb, and just then a car came barreling down on me. I was the *only* person on the corner.

The next thing I knew I felt a hand pull my sleeve and throw me down on the curb. I looked up and saw a man dressed in a business suit, carrying a briefcase. He picked me up and said, "I'm so glad I was here at that moment to help you. You would have been killed." He helped me cross the street and asked whether I would like a cup of coffee or tea. I was very shaky so I said, "Thank you, I think I would."

We went to a café close to the bus stop where I took my bus home. The man ordered us coffee. As we were drinking the coffee, I asked him where he was going, and did he work in the downtown area? He told me he was a salesman, and part of his territory was the stationery store across the street from this café. I did ask him his name, but he didn't tell me. He just smiled and said, "Your guardian angel."

After we finished our coffee, he said he had to go back to work. I thanked him again and watched him from the café as he crossed the street to the stationery store and went inside.

As I left the café, I decided to walk over to the stationery store and find out his name. I walked into the store and approached a lady behind the counter. I asked her about the salesman and explained how he had rescued me. The lady just looked at me, probably saying to herself, "Boy, is she nuts or what?"

"We have no salespeople," she said. "We order all our materials from San Francisco, and they are sent to us by United Parcel Service."

WOMAN IN THE WINDOW

MARGARET ROBERTS LYNCH

The year I was fifteen—which meant that I knew everything—was a year of transition for our household. Only my brother George and I were left at home, the other nine children having grown up and gone out on their own.

We were between houses, living with my sister Ethel until we could find a house to rent. Mom was trying to decide what she wanted to do now that most of the brood was gone.

While I was at school, Ethel and Mom would go out looking for a place for us. They finally found a lovely little house that was perched on the side of a hill. The real-estate agent couldn't get away from her office that day to show it, but she gave Mom and Ethel the key to the house so they could look at it by themselves.

When they got there, they were startled to see a woman watching them from the front window. They went up and rang the bell, but the lady just looked at them, finally turning away. Ethel and Mom were annoyed, as the agent hadn't said anyone would be there. The doors were locked so they used the key to enter. Once inside, they looked all over, calling to the lady, but the house was empty. The back door was locked from the inside. So were all the windows.

Still, Mom found the house charming, and the pair went back to the agent's office. They told her that Mom would take the house if the lady who was in the house when they got there hadn't already rented it. The agent was puzzled. She had given no one else a key. She was renting it out for an estate, and there shouldn't have been anybody there.

"What did she look like?" asked the agent. Mom described her: short, curly black hair, glasses, dark eyes. The agent paled. The house was for rent because its owner, a lady with short, curly dark hair, glasses, and dark eyes, who had been confined to the house for some time, had recently died there.

Now, my mother is afraid of nothing, least of all ghosts, and especially not afraid of a person who had apparently never harmed anyone in life. So we took the house. As I said, I was fifteen. With the typical arrogance of youth, I dismissed the story as proof that adults are truly weird, and proceeded to forget all that nonsense—until one night, about four months later.

My bedroom was at a rear back corner of the little Cape-style house, on the first floor. I really liked it because it looked out on trees—very, very close trees, as my side of the house was practically built into the hillside. One night, or perhaps it was early morning, I woke up with a feeling of being watched. I went cold. There was someone at the foot of my bed. The room was still pretty dark, but there was a sort of glow around this person, a woman in a white dress. She had—you guessed it—short, dark, curly hair and glasses.

The woman was saying something and pointing at me, but I was too terrified to hear at first. Her voice was urgent. Finally, it came through, several times, clearly and chillingly, "Leave this place, get out, get out, get out while you can. Leave this place." All the while, she was pointing at me. Her expression wasn't exactly menacing, but it was frightening.

The light went on in the room—my brother had heard voices—and she was gone. He could see that I was upset. He told me it was a nightmare, I was talking in my sleep, I was a fruitcake, and to go back to sleep. Yeah, right. I went to get Mom. She looked at me strangely, but she said only that we should think about it, and not to worry. The house had a good feeling, and the woman certainly wouldn't hurt us. Hey, I wasn't a baby. I could handle it. Still, I slept in our empty spare room, the one my brother Ray used when he came home from the navy.

That's where I was when I got up the next morning. That's where I was the next night, when a heavy rain turned torrential and drove one of the big, beautiful, very, very close trees through the window and wall of my bedroom, and right on top of my bed.

I guess I should have been grateful, but my mind refused to make the connection between the lady's visit and my narrow escape. It was just too much. It wasn't long, though, until my mom started thinking about more permanent arrangements, and we began to talk about where we should look for a house. I guess the lady must have heard us and approved of the move.

One day as my mom was talking on the phone, the doorbell started to ring. She asked the caller to hang on and went to see who was there. There was nobody, but the bell still rang. It was 10:00 a.m.; at 10:15 a.m., the bell stopped. My mom, thinking that it must be an electrical short, had one of my brothers look it over (believe me, when you have seven brothers, there's always one who can do just about any task). There was nothing wrong with the bell, he said, but he asked us to let him know if it happened again. It did. Same time, next morning—10:00 to 10:15. And again the next. I was beginning to wonder what she wanted, but my mother said she knew. Time for us to get on with our lives, she said. It wasn't for the lady's good; it was for our own. We chose a new place to live the very next day. It was the last the doorbell rang, as well. When the papers for the new place were signed, the bells stopped.

THE GHOSTLY RESTAURANT

CLIFFORD PORTER

One evening in July 1986, my wife and I were driving through downtown Spokane, Washington, looking for an inexpensive restaurant, as we were traveling with limited funds.

We came upon a place adjacent to a motel that had a special posted in the window, "Steak & Eggs, $3.85." Considering that to be quite a bargain, we stopped in. We were surprised that there was no sign on the street giving the name of the place. Still, the paper the special was painted on looked yellowed and stiff from having been there a while. The restaurant was crowded, and the greasy menus the waitress handed us looked well used. We both ordered steak and eggs.

The food was good and typical of the fare of short-order coffee shops. The help was polite and courteous. Several people got up, paid their bills, and left while we sat there. (We were later to note that no one else came in after we did.)

When our bill came, we saw that the total covered only one of the $3.85 specials; 85¢ was the charge for the other. Being honest, we pointed this out to the waitress, who promptly took the bill and said she would talk to the manager about it. She was cheerful the whole time, even when she came back and told us we didn't have to pay any more because it was her error. We paid and left. We stopped at the motel office to pick up some brochures before we drove to the home where we were staying.

We told our host couple about the restaurant. The menu had the name Chuck Wagon on it. They said that they had never heard of such a place, and it was not listed in the telephone book. When we told them the name of the motel next door to the restaurant, they were still skeptical. They said there was no restaurant there. Maybe it was new, we suggested, but it seemed as if it had been there a long time.

The next day we drove by the motel. The building was there but there was no restaurant in it. We believed from then on that we had been served dinner by angels, even if no one else does.

THE CHART

ELAINE WILLIAMS WEISS

I used to do freelance calligraphy, and often my assignment was to create and address party invitations and accessories. On this particular occasion the request was for a seating chart, a rather standard accessory at wedding dinners. The guests' names, in alphabetical order, were lettered prettily on a large chart. The florist would set the chart on a garlanded easel with lighting over it, and it held a prominent place in the foyer.

From my standpoint, the drawback was that the charts always had to be done at the very last minute. Responses were often late and sudden rearrangements happened all too often. I could do the heading beforehand, but the actual names and the layout had to wait. In this case, I had received the final version the night before the party. I assured my hostess that the chart would be in her hands the next day.

I had four lively young children, and I found it much easier to work after they were in bed for the night. There is a flow to calligraphy, and if you are interrupted midword or even midsentence, the letters can show a change, subtle as it might be.

During the day I worked on the layout and, after all were tucked in bed, I set to work. I stopped only to kiss my husband goodnight. The chart was a long list, and it was well after 3:00 a.m. when I finally laid my pens to rest. I took a last moment to proofread the names, comparing them with the typed list at my hand.

My heart sank when I got to the S's.

I had omitted a name.

There was no way to make a correction. The layout was precise: I couldn't squeeze the name in or add it at the end. Any change would be noticeable, and it would look as though the guest were an afterthought. There was no recourse except to do the whole chart over.

I was too tired to start again, so I promised myself that as soon as the children were off to school in the morning I would put the housework aside and get to the chart. And I flopped into bed and slept.

The next morning at 8:30, after the children and my husband were off and away, I received a phone call from my hostess.

"Did you finish the chart?" Her voice was agitated.

I parried. "Don't worry," I said calmly. "You'll have it today. This afternoon."

"I have to make a change," she said.

"Oh?"

"Yes." She paused. "My uncle—he died last night."

I felt a cold ribbon trickling down my spine.

"What was his name?" I asked.

Yes. Yes. Yesyesyes . . .

I never told my hostess. And I couldn't bring myself to write a list of names again for a long, long time.

SOLDIER ON THE BEACH

MICHAEL DENNIS

I was a frightened young draftee, unable to sleep, that black and mist. March night in 1969. Leaning against the shack out there on the beach, I felt my world quickly coming to an end. It was just after 3:00 a.m., and I was smoking a cigarette, listening to the China Sea lapping softly on the sand. I got a whiff of dead fish in the salty dampness, and I was dripping with sweat from the heat. The night was blacker than any I had ever seen.

This was Vietnam. I'd been there just three days, living in this tumbledown shack at a place called the Reception Center. It was where you waited for permanent assignment.

Slowly it came to me that I was not alone out there in the dark. A lone soldier was walking out of the foggy blackness along the water, coming toward me. He was in full infantryman's battle dress: badly worn jungle fatigues, crushed jungle hat, a battered rucksack with field equipment strapped to its sides, and he carried the ever-present M-16 automatic rifle. He came right up to me as if he had known I was there.

"Got a cigarette?" he asked.

"Sure," I said and held out the pack, feeling a tug as he slid out a single cigarette.

"Thanks," he said.

I offered my lighter, but he had his hands up well before I struck the flame. He then turned way around, twisting sideways and down for the light, so I didn't see his face. In retrospect, I don't believe he had one.

We spoke quietly for a few moments. He told me his unit and asked where I was going. I replied that I hadn't been assigned yet and that I was afraid of where I might end up. Then he turned to face me, but in the blackness of the night I still couldn't see his face.

"Oh, you're going to be fine, just fine. You're going to be okay," he said. His words were said with punch, real depth, and I have remembered them to this day. Overcome with emotion, I had no reply. But he seemed to understand.

"Well, gotta go," he said. "Thanks for the cigarette." He adjusted the rucksack on his back, picked up the rifle, and walked off down the beach, disappearing into the gloom.

Five months later, hurrying through an After-Action Report for my unit, talking on the phone with a clerk down at the firebase in Duc Pho, I asked about the lone soldier's unit. His calm reassurances had sustained me through some frightening times. I'd been to the Reception Center that very day, trying to recruit the best of the newly arrived soldiers for my own unit, and had been summarily thrown out by the cadre that ran the center. This was a highly restricted and secure area, they insisted. Suddenly it seemed very odd that the lone soldier had been in there, especially in battle dress, especially with a rifle, especially at 3:00 a.m., especially on the beach, especially all alone . . .

In Vietnam we always knew our calendars—we remembered dates—when we got there, when we were going home. All very important. So I knew the date of that night on the beach. The clerk down in Duc Pho looked it up—it took only a few minutes.

"You picked a hell of a date, buddy. That unit was totally wiped out that day. There was no one left alive!"

CEMETERY STORY

SUSAN M. JANSON

A widow of forty years was awakened one night by a jolt. She saw her late husband standing in the doorway, dressed in a white gown. He didn't talk but motioned with his hand to come. As she walked toward the doorway he turned and disappeared. She rarely went to the cemetery to visit his grave, but she went the next day. There she was amazed to find a fresh grave next to her husband's in the place where she was to rest in peace.

The cemetery had buried a woman in her grave by mistake.

THE FEVER

SANDRA GARDNER

I had never been a believer in ghosts. In 1972, however, I had an experience that confirmed for me that there is something supernatural out there.

We lived in a new little split-level home. Our two older sons shared a bedroom downstairs. One night I woke up and went to check on our oldest son, who had a fever and was coughing. I was sure he was getting another ear infection. I brought him upstairs and put him on the couch in the living room so I would be aware if he got any sicker, and then I returned to bed.

Two hours later I woke up from a very sound sleep. I was lying on my side and facing the hallway, which in turn faced the living room. A large, white-draped figure was standing there in the hallway. It had a dark spot where its face should have been; I sensed movement in the facial area but could not make out a face.

I thought to myself, "Well, I don't know who you are, but what do you want?" The figure raised its arm and pointed to the couch where my son lay. I thought, "I know he is there, and I am taking care of him." All of a sudden it dawned on me that I was communicating with this figure with my mind. I reached behind me, tapped my husband, and said, "You won't believe this, but there is a ghost in our hallway!" I don't remember his response, but the figure disappeared like smoke.

Within a few moments our alarm went off. I got up to check my son. He had no fever, no cough, and he said he felt great. Only two or three hours prior to that, he had been a very sick little boy.

I recalled a few days later that my sister had seen a similar figure three years ago. I called her to ask what this figure looked like. She replied, "What have you seen?" We both described exactly what we had seen, and it became clear that we had both seen the same apparition. She had awakened from a bad dream, saw the figure standing over her, and felt comfort. I know I was awake; I know what I saw. I believe that my son has a guardian angel—perhaps we all do. I wasn't scared, but I don't think I would like to see this figure again. I moved my bedroom around a few days later so I wouldn't be able to wake up and look directly into the hallway.

ANGELS

ANDREA BLASI

My family always has a story to tell me. There is one that always sticks in my mind and is my favorite. This one is no mere tale—it's the truth.

When my mom was just an infant, she had a severe case of scarlet fever. The doctor made a house call and said my mom probably wouldn't live through the night. My grandma became hysterical, but she went to church and prayed in desperation to St. Theresa, who is also known as The Little Flower. She asked for the healing of her daughter and in return she promised to dress the child up as the saint for her first communion. The doctor returned the next morning and pronounced my mom miraculously healed.

The years passed and my grandma forgot all about the promise she had made in a prayer long ago. The night before her first communion, my mom went to bed with her beautiful, new white dress hanging in the closet. My grandma also went to bed, only to be rudely awakened by a ghostly figure at the foot of her bed.

It was the image of St. Theresa, and she was calling out, "Remember your promise, Victoria."

My grandma got up quickly, dressed, and made a late-night visit to the convent. She explained the story to the nuns and begged them for the material and pattern for the outfit. My grandma, who was a seamstress, then stayed up all night and well into the morning, sewing for the communion that evening.

The outfit consisted of a long, white, sacklike garment covering the arms, neck, and legs. There was also a long veil to be worn on the head. So it was an understatement to say my mom looked a little different from the other children there.

The man who was organizing the ceremony took one look at my mom and told her she had to walk in the very back of the line. When the priest saw my mom, however, he insisted that she lead the procession into the church.

The church was in a tiny town in Pennsylvania where everyone knew everyone else. When my mom walked down the aisle, a stranger in a blue suit walked into the church and up to my mom, and, though it was the cold, snowy month of February, handed her two dozen pure-white roses. He then proceeded to leave the church and was never seen or heard from again.

MORNING GHOST

HILDA FERREIRA-ROBICHAUD

In the summer of 1977, my husband and I traveled to Canada for our first vacation as newlyweds. My husband's family is originally from a small village outside of Harvey, New Brunswick, and we decided to visit John's paternal grandmother, Jane Blunt, there. She had lived in a small farmhouse on one hundred acres of land since 1949.

John and I stayed with Jane for our entire two-week vacation. One morning as we all sat down to breakfast, Jane was reminded of the story of the morning ghost. "The morning ghost?" I questioned. She went on to tell us this true story as we sat motionless in our chairs, hanging on every word. She first explained that some people on her road had actually seen the ghost, and that she had heard about the ghost from her brother-in-law, Martin Blunt. He lived on the one hundred acres of land next to Jane. He also lived adjacent to the vacant Thomasson property.

Jane told us that the ghost began to appear on Martin's property at the beginning of the summer of 1951, and, according to Martin, the ghost would appear only in the morning, at about five o'clock. The apparition was a young woman, approximately thirty years old, who could be seen behind the cedar rail fence that divided the Thomasson property from his. She would be at the same location each and every day, dressed in a long, flowing, white nightgown, and then move onto Martin's lot.

Martin first saw the ghost early one morning as he walked from his house to the barn to milk his cows. Initially, he could not, quite literally, believe his eyes. In the next moments he came to the realization that the white, glowing figure by the fence was something extraordinary. But what was it?

The woman appeared to rise up from the Thomasson property, float over the wooden fence, and onto Martin's property. Martin remembered the stories his mother had told him about spirits and ghosts when he was a youngster; his mother was a very religious and superstitious woman who believed strongly in the unexplained and supernatural. He had never actually believed in spirits and spooks before, but he knew that he was looking at a genuine ghost. He stared at the vision for a long time—it seemed like an eternity. He just couldn't keep his eyes off this incredible sight. Finally the woman turned away and began walking down the path alongside the fence and into the woods in back of Martin's land. Martin's eyes were still fixed on the ghost as she disappeared from sight.

Martin proceeded to go into the barn to milk the cows, as he did every morning. This morning was unlike every morning, however, for he was still shocked by what he had witnessed, and he continued to be for many days thereafter. He didn't dare tell anyone in his family what he had witnessed. They might think he was out of his mind.

A few days later Martin became ill with the flu and his fifteen-year-old son, Isaac, took over the chore of milking the cows. Trudging down the path to the barn, Isaac also saw the apparition at the cedar fence. He turned, raced back to the house, and dashed up the bedroom stairs to tell his father what he had just seen.

Martin listened to Isaac's story and decided to confess that he had seen the same ghost. He also admitted that he felt relieved to hear that he wasn't the only one who saw her. Isaac was both frightened and curious and said that he had watched the ghost walk alongside the fence until she disappeared. It was then that Isaac and Martin decided they would follow the apparition and see where she would lead. They were both anxious about this undertaking but refused to show each other their fear.

Martin began to feel just like his mother must have felt when she had told him her ghost stories. His mother had once told him that if a spirit is held to the earth, that spirit is not at rest nor at peace. It is not of this world, and it is not of the next world. The earthbound spirit is troubled and, until its pain can be soothed, it cannot be free of the earth. Funny how his mother's philosophy had stayed with him all of those years.

The next morning Martin and Isaac arose at 4:00 a.m., a bit earlier than usual, and set off to milk the cows. They finished the milking and waited until five o'clock for the ghost to reappear at the fence. Five o'clock arrived and the morning ghost appeared, as usual. The two ghost trackers were anxious; both had lumps in their throats and knots in their stomachs. They proceeded to follow the figure as she led them into the woods. Martin decided that they would stay about fifty feet behind the ghost. He thought it odd that the woman did not notice that she was being followed, but Isaac thought maybe she wanted them to follow her.

The morning ghost walked along the fence until she came to the last post. Then she turned suddenly, walking deeper into the woods and onto the Thomasson property, following a deer path that led to a shallow stream. She stopped at the stream, knelt down on the grassy bank, and put her transparent white hand into the water. She next placed her hand beside a large rock next to the bank and tried unsuccessfully to lift it. Isaac and Martin watched in confusion, wondering what she was trying to do. After much effort trying to lift the huge rock, the ghostly woman gave up her efforts, pulled her hands from the water, stood up, cupped her hands over her face, and began crying.

Martin and Isaac felt sorry for the woman, but they didn't know what to do. They noticed that they could not hear her crying. After a while she took her hands from her face slowly and turned toward Martin and Isaac. She stared straight at them both. The pair realized that the ghost knew they were following her. Isaac became so frightened that he ran away as fast as he could.

Martin and the ghost stared at one another. Martin stayed because he wasn't afraid of the ghost anymore. He knew she was not going to harm him. The woman seemed very sad and alone, and Martin tried to ask her whether she needed his help. But the ghost only looked down into the icy water of the stream; then she faded into the sunlight.

Martin called out to his son to come back, as the ghost was no longer there. He explained to Isaac that the ghost had tried to tell him something but that he didn't know what it was. Isaac and Martin searched the stream for clues and spent an hour looking for the large rock that the ghost had tried to turn over. Finally Isaac found it. Underneath the rock was a small black object. It was a handgun. Martin reached down to pick it up. It was a rusted .38 caliber revolver that looked as though it had been in the water for years.

Martin immediately took the revolver to the nearest Mounted Police headquarters. He hoped he could get some answers to this mystery. Martin told Officer Chatham that he had found the gun in the stream on the old Thomasson farm. The officer inspected the gun for a serial number that might tell him to whom the gun belonged. The gun was registered to James Thomasson, who had reported the gun stolen about a month before his wife Mathilda was found dead. The officer thought it rather odd that the gun should turn up twenty years after the murder.

Martin asked many questions about Mrs. Thomasson's murder. Officer Chatham read from his records and told Martin that they had never found the murder weapon or caught the killer. The victim had been found just outside her house in her nightclothes, very near the railing that surrounded the farm. She was covered in blood and had been shot in the head. Mr. Thomasson had discovered the body after coming home from a hunting trip the same morning.

Martin also learned that she had died around five o'clock in the morning. His eyes grew wide with astonishment. He thought to himself, That's the same time the ghost appears every morning! The ghost must be Mathilda Thomasson, and she's trying to tell me who killed her.

Martin asked what had happened to James Thomasson. The officer said that Thomasson had moved out of town after his wife died. It seemed his wife left him quite a bit of money. Martin asked whether Mr. Thomasson was ever a suspect in the shooting. The officer explained that he was never a suspect because he had returned from hunting that day. He couldn't have killed his wife. Martin pleaded with the officer to talk with Thomasson.

When Officer Chatham tracked down Thomasson and showed him the missing handgun, Thomasson immediately confessed to his wife's murder. He claimed that he had felt guilty all these years for killing his wife and taking her money and that he had to clear his conscience.

The next morning Martin watched for the appearance of Mrs. Thomasson's ghost at five o'clock. She appeared just like always, but this time she didn't walk down the path and into the woods. This morning she stayed by the cedar fence and no longer had a sad expression on her face. She was smiling. Martin knew that her spirit would finally be released and that her soul would be at peace now that her murder was solved.

Martin suspected that this would be the last time that he would see the familiar ghost. He was happy that he had helped, yet sad to see her go. But more than that he wanted to get back to his uneventful life of farming without being bothered by any more ghosts.

SNOW GHOST, OR 'S NO GHOST

JONES BARNETT

John Steinbeck is reported to have once said, "I do not believe in ghosts, although I have seen them." I myself believe in them thoroughly, although I have never seen one.

My encounter happened while traveling through the northwestern states in the winter of 1950 with my wife, our two-year-old daughter, and not much else—you couldn't call a 1939 Plymouth coupe much of anything. Wind was swishing curtains of very dry snow across the streets in Denver as I paid the service station attendant for filling our tank. He also added some antifreeze to the carburetor and put in a quart of oil. He noticed my license plates with the bucking horse emblem and said,"If you're looking for a place to put up for the night, there's a motel just down the highway half a mile from here." I thanked him, got into the Plymouth, and started off toward the highway. The tiny amount of warm air that the little heater struggled to fan out wasn't really sufficient, but my wife and daughter were able to keep warm with blankets tucked around them.

I was young and not long ago had been discharged from the service. I believed myself to be thoroughly able to accomplish anything I set out to do. My primary reason for not staying the night in Denver was that I had had to spend more money keeping the Plymouth running than I had planned. I had already had fuel-pump and carburetor problems. If this kept up, I wouldn't have enough money left to make it the rest of the way to Sheridan, Wyoming. I took a chance; now I doubt the wisdom of taking chances when other people's lives are at stake.

The snow seemed to be coming up from the highway in a sweeping arc. Visibility was about fifteen feet as the white sheets hit the windshield. I thought I would be able to see better when we left the glare of the city lights. And the storm had to let up its ferocious onslaught soon, I reasoned. I kept going, but not too fast; the best I could do was thirty miles per hour. Sometimes I would have to slow down to a complete standstill until the wind dropped and I could see again.

My wife and baby were sleeping. I would have been drowsy too if I had not been so tense. My watch showed it was two in the morning. We were probably not more than a hundred miles outside of Denver when the car grew colder and the windshield froze over. I could not tell whether we were in the center of the road or in the oncoming traffic's lane. If we were in the wrong lane and a truck came along, we'd certainly be hit. I stopped and rolled down my window to better see the road. Strong gusts of wind shook the car like a toy. Why hadn't we stayed in Denver? I could have called my boss to send money. Man, this was dumb.

I raced the engine to increase the heater's tiny output. That's when it happened. The motor started flooding, coughed, and quit. Stone-cold dead. How long could people survive in a blizzard like this? Sure, stay in the car, everyone knows that. But people are found frozen to death in cars all the time.

My wife woke up and asked, "What's wrong?" I tried to act confident. "Carburetor flooded again. I'll fix it." I couldn't fix it, and I knew it. "I'm going to wait until this wind lets up a little."

She said, "You can fix it." Then she pulled the blankets closer about herself and the baby, while I sat there at a complete loss as to what to do next. I am not an automobile mechanic—never have been.

The bone-chilling cold was creeping in. I heard a sound above the wind. A voice? We had not passed another car or seen a sign of life in hours. I roused myself and listened. There again. Something at the window. I looked out the black glass, straining my eyes. Nothing. No light. No vehicle. Then the hood of the Plymouth went up. The wind? I've got to get out and close the hood before the gale tears it away, I thought.

I stepped out into the storm to glimpse what appeared to be a shadowy figure bent over the fender, peering under the hood. Snow driven by icy wind blinded my eyes, but I could hear the sounds of a screwdriver or a wrench. Then the hood lowered and I heard a disembodied voice say, "Try it now. Try your starter." I hit the starter and the little engine sputtered and picked up a rhythm. I got out again to thank my benefactor. No one was there. Back inside my car, I shifted to first gear, let out the clutch, and forged ahead into the elements. I did not pass a single car, or even a lighted farmhouse, for miles.

When my wife next awoke, I had parked in front of a service station at an all-night café. We went inside for breakfast. The snowplows were out now, and we could soon be on our way again. She said to me, "You know, I never knew you to be able to fix anything on a car. But you did come through in an emergency, didn't you?"

She doesn't know to this day that I didn't fix the car that snowy night.

I've still never seen a ghost. But they exist.

THE BEGGAR

MARY BALLANTYNE

One of my high school classmates—a quiet boy, not one of the "in" crowd—electrified our social studies class with the following story. Though it has been thirty years, I can almost hear his voice that day:

"One Fourth of July weekend my family and friends were having a huge picnic on the banks of the Russian River. Everyone was having a great time, and it was really crowded.

"Suddenly someone let out a scream, and when I looked I saw my little sister, who was about eighteen months old, floating facedown in the river! She was dragged out immediately and the fire department arrived quickly. As we all gathered around, watching the firemen take turns giving mouth-to-mouth resuscitation, I saw one fireman look at one of his comrades and, slowly, almost imperceptibly, shake his head.

"I was standing on top of one of the picnic tables so that I could see better, when I felt a pulling on my pantleg. I looked down and saw an old, thin, raggedy man. He wasn't dirty, like a hobo, but his clothes were cheap, old, and torn. He asked me, 'May I have some bread from your table?'

"I was amazed that he could have the insensitivity to beg when my sister was dying, maybe dead already, but I told him to help himself, mostly just to be rid of him. Somewhere in the back of my head I realized that we had enormous amounts of food and could certainly spare him some bread. I guess the man helped himself and left immediately, because when I looked again, seconds later, he was gone.

"Then I heard someone in the crowd yell out, 'Yea!' Suddenly everyone in sight was starting to jump up and down with joy: my little sister had started breathing again! What a relief! Everyone was crying and giving prayers of thanks and, well, it just turned out to be quite a day all around.

"That night as I slept the old man who had spoken to me at the picnic came to me in my dream, but he was wearing fine velvet robes and said to me, 'You will find me in El Libro de Santos.' It was a very vivid dream.

"The next day was Sunday, and as we were all devout Catholics, and as we all had something extra fine to thank God for, we headed off to church. All during the service I couldn't get that old man out of my mind. So as my family was filing out, I went to the priest's office and asked him if he knew what 'El Libro de Santos' was.

"He told me it is *The Book of Saints* in Spanish and said he was sure it was there somewhere. He scanned the bookshelf and with a little 'Ah, ha!' he reached up and pulled down a very large, beautifully bound tome. He put it on his desk and invited me to help myself.

"Eagerly, but carefully, I began to turn the pages. There were so many portraits of great men and women. I didn't recognize any of them and couldn't read any of the Latin captions, but I knew these people were saintly. (I must say that more than once in those moments I felt rather foolish looking in this book because a dream had told me to.) But I persevered. And *finally*—there he was! There could be no mistaking it.

Here was a picture of the man in my dream—the exact image of the beggar at Russian River!

"Breathlessly I asked the priest who this man was. The father looked at the caption and said, 'Why, that's St. Clement I, the patron saint of the drowned.' "

A HAUNTED TREE

RICK KAUFMAN

I had flown to Arkansas to attend the wedding of my youngest brother. The day following the wedding, my brother and his new wife took me around to see the sights, which included a trip to Fayetteville, about twenty miles away.

It was a beautiful June day, with blue sky, bright sun, and gentle breezes. We walked around the town, visiting the University of Arkansas campus and seeing some of the more notable town buildings.

I took quite a few pictures and was soon low on film, so we headed in the direction of a local camera store. I recall the three of us chatting as we walked slowly down a tree-lined street. About halfway down the block, as we were passing underneath one of the trees, I felt myself shudder and inexplicably said to my brother and his wife: "This tree should not be standing; let's hurry and get out from under it!"

The tree in question looked identical to the other twenty or thirty trees on the block; it was some fifty or sixty feet tall, with thick branches and trunk, and sported a dense coat of green leaves. Why I felt and said what I did, I don't know, but I remember feeling a sense of relief as we passed beyond the reach of its outstretched limbs. Needless to say, my remarks drew quizzical looks and comments from my two companions, but we nevertheless hurried on our way.

We finally found the camera store, which was located at the end of the block where the tree-lined street came to a dead end. We entered the store, I did my shopping, and we left within about five minutes. I remember being disoriented as I came back outside because instead of seeing the long street we had just come down, there was a short street ending in a green mountain or hill. It took but an instant to realize what we were actually looking at—the very tree that had evoked my shudder and alarm stood no more. Within the space of a couple of minutes, it had indeed fallen and was now lying across the street, blocking traffic and obscuring the view behind it.

I was stunned and amazed, as were my companions. Not only had this really happened but I had somehow sensed that it was about to happen and had realized we would be in peril if we lingered too long.

We walked the shortened block to the tree, which was now attracting police vehicles and spectators. Fortunately, no one had been injured, nor was anything damaged. Our quick and inexpert inspection revealed nothing unusual about the tree, other than the fact that most of it was now lying on its side. Because I was sightseeing with my camera, and of course had my newly purchased film, I was able to record for posterity the tree that had somehow communicated with me.

GRANNY'S DRESS

TERI BARBER SHARUM

Granny's house, a rambling two-story structure that had seen better days, sat on the edge of the historic district in Fort Smith, Arkansas. It was a modest home with none of the fancy Victorian features that would qualify it as a place of historical interest or cause one to think of it as anything but a decent rental house. But Granny was proud of it.

She lived in the attic.

At least, that's what Dan and Glenn and Tom, the guys who rented the house, told me shortly after they moved in. They heard her rocking. They heard the click of knitting needles at odd hours. And sometimes they heard a soft, sweet chuckle drifting down the stairs.

Dan, my boyfriend, said that Granny was our guardian angel. Lord knows, we needed a guardian angel, so why not Granny? She was quiet and gentle and didn't seem to be offended by the constant drifting in and out of the long-haired boys and barefoot girls who hung out in her living room.

I liked the idea of a benevolent ghost living in my boyfriend's attic, but I didn't take it seriously. Not even when I heard the creak of her rocking chair. Not even when I saw her.

One night as I stood alone at the top of the stairs, a formless white shape, slightly taller than I, hovered by my right shoulder. I turned to look at her, but she was gone. A puff of cigarette smoke, I thought, though I wasn't smoking.

"I saw Granny," I whispered to Dan when I got downstairs. "I think she was sizing me up."

Granny seemed partial to boys; none of the girls who visited her house had ever seen or heard her. None but I.

"She likes you, Angel," Dan said, "almost as much as I do."

Rentals, relationships, and guardian angels can't last forever. I stopped by to see Dan the day the guys moved out of Granny's house.

"We have a present for you," he said, handing me a small brown box with a dilapidated bow stuck on the top.

I eagerly opened the box and pulled out a blue-purple silk dress and jacket that were at least fifty years old.

"They're beautiful," I said, my eyes wide and misty.

"We think Granny wants you to have them," Dan said. "We found them in the attic. Go try them on."

I hesitated, knowing the dress wouldn't fit—dresses never fit me as they were supposed to. I was short-waisted, short-legged, small-chested, and big-hipped. And the dress had straps, which couldn't possibly stay on my sloping shoulders.

"It'll fit," he said, so I reluctantly went into the bathroom and prepared to prove to him that it wouldn't.

I slipped the dress over my head and got ready to struggle with the side zipper. No struggle—the zipper pulled the worn silk snugly against my side, and the waist closed just where *my* waist was. Tiny silver stars, embroidered all over the dress, fell smoothly across my hips down to just below my ankles. The straps sat softly on my shoulders, after I tucked in a little extra flap of fabric.

"What is this?" I wondered aloud. I examined the flap and realized that the straps had been taken up a couple of inches to accommodate both my short-waistedness and my rounded shoulders.

I put the jacket on to try to cover my goose bumps and went into the kitchen to model Granny's dress.

"It fits as if it was made for me," I said.

"Maybe it was," Dan said. "The night you saw her on the stairs, standing at your shoulder, you said she was sizing you up. . . ."

One warm autumn night some fifteen years later, when I was in need of a guardian angel, I thought about Granny. I wondered whether she still watched over Dan and Glenn and Tom. I wondered about the dress, which was safely stored in my attic. I wondered . . .

I heard noises—a creaking, the sound of cardboard scraping open, the rustle of fabric unfolding. I tiptoed from the bedroom.

She stood at the head of the stairs, cloaked in blue-purple silk with tiny silver stars. In the instant that I gazed at her, she was gone.

"A puff of smoke," I said, stubbing out my cigarette. "Nothing more than a puff of smoke."

WHERE SPIRITS DWELL

THE HAUNTED HOMESTEAD

MARTHA GEISSINGER

Our search for a new home began when we were expecting a new baby. We looked at several houses, but not one of them was what I was searching for. It was a blisteringly hot day when we decided to look at a house I had always admired but never really thought we could afford. The outside of the house was perfect; it had a big porch and a weeping willow tree in the yard, and it sat away from the surrounding neighbors. Woods encircled the property.

As we walked into the house, I knew this was the one. Without really seeing any more than the living room, I was sure I knew how the rest of the house was laid out. I was obsessed with having this property and told my husband I didn't want to look any further. A few months later the house belonged to us. The house was truly beautiful; we couldn't have asked for anything more.

Our rather strange experiences began on the day we moved. It was a dark, gloomy, rainy day. As soon as we started moving our things in, a hostile and nasty attitude seemed to overcome the members of our family. At first I attributed this to the hardship we all felt because of the move and figured we would all feel better after we were settled.

Our first encounter with what I will refer to as "the spirit" came one evening while we were watching television. I heard a noise coming from

97

the kitchen and went to see what it was. The knob on the door to the basement was turning; it was almost as if someone was trying to get out but the door was stuck. All the children were in the living room, so I thought maybe it was someone trying to break in after getting entry through the basement. Terrified, I reached for the doorknob and flung open the door, but nobody was there. Slowly I entered the basement, but there was no sign of anyone. That night my husband placed a bolt on the basement entry and a chain on the door to the basement.

We brushed off this encounter and continued our daily routines. Then one drizzly night I sat alone watching television—I remember that I had my back to the kitchen—when I suddenly felt as if I wasn't alone. Before I knew it, I felt a hand touch my head. At first I thought it was one of my daughters touching me as she passed by, but as I turned to face the kitchen I saw a ghostly figure dart quickly toward the basement door. I don't know what possessed me at this point, but I got up and walked to the basement door and opened it. There was nothing there. At this point I said, aloud, to the spirit that I knew he or she existed. I told it that I was willing to share my home and would welcome its presence if it would leave us alone. I even told it I would call it George, though I really had no idea if it was a male or a female. I thought that George was a good name for a ghost.

Rather than scare my children, I kept this encounter to myself, but I also felt safe and at home, sure that George and I had made a pact. Time passed and we always heard a lot of strange and unexplained knocks, thumps, and footsteps. We had items disappear and reappear at various times. I remember on one occasion a friend had brought a cassette over for me to hear, and we placed it near the stereo. When we went to pick it up, it was gone. We searched for about an hour and a half and then, mysteriously, there it was where we had originally placed it. I attributed this to one of George's playful pranks. On occasion things would fall off the walls or shelves for no reason; oddly enough, they never broke. Sometimes at night I could hear a child talking and crying. My oldest daughter always said she never felt alone in her room; friends who came to spend the night would say the same thing.

But everyone seemed to change after we moved in. We all seemed unhappy, became inexplicably sick more frequently, and there were growing tensions in my marriage. Eventually my husband and I divorced. I had to hire live-in baby-sitters, who also seemed to become nasty, and they started having bad things happen to them. One sitter left saying that the house was possessed.

Eventually the home became more than I could handle, and I made the decision to let the mortgage company foreclose on it. During the past four years not only had my husband and I divorced but my oldest daughter had left home and my middle daughter had moved out and in with her father. I no longer felt the need to keep the house I had once loved.

It was about this time that the bangs and footsteps became more frequent. One night after the sun had set, I heard a loud bang within the house. Because I was alone with two small children, I telephoned the police, who came and searched everywhere but could find nothing that would have caused the noise.

For four years, the door to the attic had been propped open with a big barrel. The wood in the door was almost an inch thick, and the door itself was about six feet tall and four feet wide. There was no way anyone could shut it without me knowing it. One night my daughter and I heard a big bang that shook the house. We discovered that the attic door was closed. Neither of us was strong enough to open it, so we had to wait for my boyfriend to come over. When he opened it, we discovered that the barrel had been moved from one place to another; no one could have moved it without locking himself in the attic. I truly believe that this was the work of George once again.

I lay in bed one night and could hear the child crying again, and then I heard the sound of a rocking chair rocking and the crying stopped.

Just before I moved, my boyfriend and I were upstairs when we heard a noise in the kitchen. It was as if someone had fallen on the floor. A few seconds later we heard footsteps. As they came closer to the stairs, I told my boyfriend to get the gun and load it. I was sure someone had broken in. We waited as I counted the footsteps, but when they reached the top of the stairs and we got out of bed and threw open the bedroom door, nothing was to be seen.

About a week later I was chatting on the phone when I heard a large bang and I assumed one of my kids had knocked something over. But to my surprise, my kids ran in screaming, "What was that?" Just then I heard footsteps and panicked and phoned the police. As usual we could find nothing that had fallen and nobody who could have created the footsteps. By now I swore I was losing my sanity.

The day of the move finally arrived—a dark, gloomy, rainy day. I moved most of my belongings that day, but because my son was ill, I quit early and decided to continue the next day. I left my answering machine on, with a number where I could be reached.

The next day when I returned to the house, there had been no calls. About a week later, some friends came to see me. One friend said he had gone to our home on the night I had left, and that he had seen a dark-haired lady there who wouldn't answer the door. I had nothing packed up in the living room that would in any way have resembled a dark-haired lady. I wondered whether this could have been my ghost.

Another friend recalled telephoning me that same evening and said a woman had answered the phone and stated that I was gone for the evening but would be back. Could this have been the woman my other friend had seen?

The strange happenings in this house were never explained. I returned on one occasion to secure the door, and at that time I took pictures. One picture seems to show a figure suspended in air and a tombstone outside one window. Strangely, the figure was outside looking in. Another photo showed the face of a man staring into the house.

Rumor has it that every family who lived there experienced a series of tragedies. Are these just coincidences, or are they the work of an unknown spirit who has roamed the property for years?

THE HOODED FIGURE

DEBORAH PRATT

I was never a kid who was afraid of the dark or of being alone. So on the night my mother had to go out to pick up my sister at the train station,

I was content to stay home by myself. I had washed my hair and, lacking today's convenience of a hair dryer, I sat in front of the living-room fireplace to dry it.

I guess I was daydreaming a bit when I suddenly felt what seemed like very light and gentle fingers being run through my hair. I glanced up quickly to the mirror hung over the fireplace and saw a figure dressed completely in black with a hood over its head. I was a bit surprised but not frightened. I was immediately impressed with his hands, which were long, delicate, and beautiful.

In the next instant he realized I could see him. He glanced up toward the mirror and appeared startled. All I could see of his face were his nose, cheekbones, lips, and chin, which were highlighted in the firelight. He was a young man, maybe in his early twenties. The next moment he vanished.

When my mother returned I waited until we were alone and I carefully asked a few questions. I knew my mother could "see" spirits, but I had been warned at an early age not to talk about it. When I mentioned seeing a hooded figure dressed in black, she became very quiet and rather guarded. She quietly asked where I had seen this figure.

I did not want to worry her or cause her to think I was in any danger. I knew I wasn't. I told her of the times as a small child I had seen these figures in the old gardens. She relaxed a bit and told me this: Long ago there had been a monastery built on the land where our house now stood. The monks belonged to an order that had taken vows of poverty and silence. They had planted the beautiful fruit trees and gardens that surrounded the house, which were now neglected. It seems the monks' vows were broken one by one over the years and the place prospered. At some point there was a terrible fire and many of them died in the flames. The natives said it was a "judgment of God" and I gather no more was said.

The house still stands although another family owns it now. I still often wonder if they ever see the monks in the garden.

A DRINK OF WATER

DAVID N. COOPER

About a month after I moved to a new apartment that I had subleased from a couple eager to move, I came home from work one night (after 1:00 a.m., as usual) to find the water running in the bathroom sink. My first thought, of course, was that I had been absentminded and had left the water running as I had hurried to leave for work.

A few weeks later, I came home again at night to find the water in the kitchen sink running full blast. I thought that this was odd because surely I would have noticed the kitchen faucet running. After further thought, I realized I had not been in the kitchen area that evening and therefore would have had no opportunity to even touch the kitchen faucet.

Maybe a week had gone by when a similar situation occurred. This time a chair had been moved in my living room (away from the wall), and the water was running in the bathtub.

It was only a few days after this last incident that I was lying on the bed in the bedroom in the back of the apartment, about to fall asleep. It was earlier than usual since I had not had to work that night. From the front room of the apartment, I heard, as plain as could be, a small child ask, "Daddy, could I have a drink of water?"

Being half asleep and half awake, I lay there in bed trying to rationalize what I had just heard. Was it my imagination? Was it coming from next door? I was now awake. And I heard it again. "Daddy, could I have a drink of water?"

To get to sleep that night I had to rationalize: though what I had heard was as clear as day and seemed to be coming from the front room of my apartment, it must have been coming through the wall from either the apartment on my immediate right or on my immediate left.

Two days later, in front of our building, I met the neighbor who lived on my immediate right. I took a chance and asked her whether the visitors had left. When she asked me point blank, "What visitors?" I explained about hearing the small child ask for a drink of water.

It turned out that, though nothing strange was happening in her apartment, her boyfriend—whose apartment was to the immediate left of mine—was experiencing similar episodes. He was hearing the child ask for a drink of water. His water was being turned on mysteriously in the middle of the night. His furniture was being moved around.

Needless to say, I didn't stay long in that apartment after my close encounter was corroborated. But whatever the presence was, it obviously meant no harm to anyone. All the child wanted was a drink of water.

THE MRS. SHORTER STORY

STAR NOVAK-BROYLES

Our ghost story begins in the fall of 1990 when we started to remodel the living room of our old, rambling, two-story house. My husband had removed layers of crumbling, faded wallpaper, and he was knocking out laths and old concrete before putting up new plasterboard. We had our furniture covered, and our television set was on a rolling stand so it could be maneuvered easily.

My husband had unplugged the television set and had rolled it out of the way. He was involved in his work when he became aware that the television was on, and that it was switching channels on its own. Suddenly it went off, and my husband didn't know what to think. He decided, however, not to tell me what had happened.

A few nights later as I lay reading in bed, I dozed off with the light still on. Suddenly I was awakened by a bright flash of light that seemed to travel toward me from the corner of the bedroom. It made a popping sound as it disappeared a few inches from my face. I sat straight up in bed, and I looked around to see whether the light behind my bed was still on and intact. I had no explanation, and I reasoned to myself that I had been dreaming.

The next night we were both asleep in the bedroom. My husband woke up about 2:00 a.m. and wondered why he was awake. Suddenly the bright light appeared, as it had the night before, and my husband saw it moving toward me from the corner of the bedroom. I was startled awake by a light, which popped in front of my face, and then it was gone. "What was that? Did a light bulb pop?" I asked. My husband calmly told me to go back to sleep; it was nothing.

The following morning on our way to work, my husband described in detail the event of the night before. I was so surprised that his description of the strange light exactly matched the encounter I had had but hadn't told him about. We both thought that it was very strange, and we agreed to keep our eyes open around the house.

Some friends at work told us that we might have had an encounter with a ghost, and this was the spirit's way of getting our attention. I started to research some of the history of our house and found that it had been moved to its present location from about two blocks away in the late 1950s. From speaking to some of the older folks in the community and visiting the library to read old newspapers, I came across some interesting facts, most notably that the house was occupied by the Shorter family; Mrs. Shorter had died unexpectedly from a heart attack in our living room. She was in her fifties, and this happened some time in the 1940s.

Sometimes, while walking around the house, I would notice the most wonderful scent of a fresh apple pie baking—and we had not even turned the oven on. Other times I detected the scent of someone's grandmother's perfume, the kind of lilac or rose water that was popular in the forties. The scent seemed to follow me through the house. Still other times I would sit in my bedroom, worried or concerned about some problem, and I would feel as though a blanket were being placed around my shoulders. The feelings were always comforting, and I was never scared. Once, upon coming home from work, I was "greeted" at the door by what looked like a hundred tiny sparkles (which a medium we consulted later told me was our spirit welcoming me home).

I also know that our ghost had a playful side, too. Personal objects would turn up missing in the morning and reappear a day or two later in another location, or right where I had left them in the first place. Strange noises and footsteps in the middle of the night, glimpses of a shadow that passed silently into another room, and cool, unexplained breezes were also signs that a ghost was with us.

Eventually we contacted a medium who agreed to come to our house. Immediately upon arriving, she confirmed that we indeed had a ghost and that there were not one, but three, ghosts in our home! She felt their presence, and I told her about some of the incidents that had happened. She was very excited as she told us that the ghost who'd been calling attention to herself just wanted to be known. We placed a tape recorder in one of our upstairs rooms, loaded the recorder with a new blank tape, lit a candle, and told the spirit that this was her chance to communicate with us. We were all downstairs at the time of the taping, with the doors closed so that no one could enter the upstairs floor. Later we listened intently to the tape, and to my complete surprise a woman's voice was heard to say "Thank you." I decided right then to call our ghost Mrs. Shorter, because I was fairly sure that this was indeed her.

Over the days and weeks that followed, I would enter my bedroom and feel her presence and smell her grandmotherly smell. I would talk to her, as the medium had suggested, and it soothed my uneasy feelings. She was an unseen friend, a presence, and I came to enjoy her.

Suddenly she left our home. Our living room had long been remodeled. I was sad, but glad that she could continue her journey—the medium had told me that sometimes spirits get trapped between their physical lives and spiritual lives, and they continue to wander back and forth, kind of like lost souls, always searching.

We did have one other encounter that was very strange. A woman innocently called us and asked to speak to Mrs. Shorter. My husband told her that she must have the wrong number, and he didn't think twice about the call.

A few nights later my husband answered the phone and the same woman again asked for Mrs. Shorter. He told her that she had a wrong number. The phone immediately rang again, and I picked up the receiver. The woman asked once again for Mrs. Shorter, and I politely explained to her that no Mrs. Shorter lived here. "What number are you trying to call?" I asked. The phone number the woman recited was indeed ours, but the woman insisted that she had the correct number. She told us that it was in the phone book. Indeed, listed in the city's 1989 directory under "Shorter, K." was our phone number, and we'd had our new phone number only a few months. And the address listed was two blocks away—the very lot that our house had occupied in the 1950s. It was very peculiar, and I have not yet figured it out. Was it perhaps Mrs. Shorter's way of letting me know that she had passed on? Would she return? Was she trying to contact me?

Months have passed, and we have just started to remodel another room in our house. Suddenly we are hearing new sounds and feeling new sensations, and since we have just started this project, we're not sure what we have uncovered. Perhaps it is another ghost trying to catch our attention—after all, the medium did say that we have *three* ghosts coinhabiting our home!

THE BUILDING WITH A PAST

VERONICA V. TIPTON

In the late 1960s our family purchased a really neat old structure—built in 1868 in a small, seaside California town. It was constructed by early shipwrights in a Nantucket style out of redwood, and originally it was a boardinghouse. After some years it became one of the town's bordellos. It was operated as such until 1962, according to a local retired deputy sheriff. He made his last raid there in that year.

When my husband, Dick, and I purchased the place, it had become a respectable antique shop and art gallery. We planned to continue these types of operations and also intended to live in the building, which had a gorgeous view of the water and of all the ship traffic entering the strait.

After much restoration and extensive cleaning, we moved in and opened up shop. Dick and I had the madam's quarters, pink-tiled bath and all, and our two daughters had all of the upstairs rooms for bedrooms, studies, and playroom. Dick had a combination office-darkroom and I had an office. *We did not believe in ghosts!* Never even thought about them.

One afternoon I returned to the shop to find our employee hiding in a corner. She insisted that a woman continued to walk toward her from the back hallway and then disappeared. I searched the building but found nothing. We went through this routine several times. Finally the employee quit because, as she put it, "I can't handle a spook." I thought that she had a problem.

The new employee I hired never mentioned seeing anything unusual, but then she was kind of "supernatural" herself. All seemed quiet for a while until one morning at seven when the dog and I returned from our usual walk and started upstairs to my office, our daily routine.

Before we even made it to the first landing, the dog backed down the stairs, snarling, ears flat against her head, frightened and angry. I attempted to coax her up with me, but she refused to move. I grabbed a baseball bat and checked out all of the seven rooms and the closets and the bathroom. I found nothing except a puddle in front of my office door. I realized that our tough English bullterrier had followed me as far as my office at the end of the hall and had become so upset that she urinated. The dog never again went beyond the first landing. It took a while for my spine to warm up that morning.

Soon after that experience our daughters started sitting down at the breakfast table each morning and beginning their conversation with their father with a question such as "Did you walk downstairs about midnight last night?" When his answer was negative, they glanced at each other. I didn't think much about it until the dog and I were home alone one evening. Suddenly she awakened, looked around, leaped from her chair, and charged at something. She chased whatever it was to the back door and did not quiet down for at least an hour.

One day as a friend was enjoying a drink by the open Dutch door, he casually remarked, "Did you see that ghost pass by?" I thought that he was kidding. He wasn't. He wasn't really concerned because unusual things occurred in his own house periodically. My husband also noticed something pass by, though he pretended that he didn't.

We decided to move out and convert the entire building to commercial use. All of the upstairs rooms were rented out to small shopkeepers, and we turned the madam's quarters into a restaurant. A security alarm with a motion detector and entry pads was installed and connected directly to the police station. Every morning when I arrived at work, I dashed to turn off the alarm and walked down the hall to unlock the side door.

Each morning I heard footsteps on the stairs as I approached. I tried to believe that it was just the old building creaking. As I worked in the kitchen, however, and listened to the footsteps in the hall overhead, I knew it wasn't the wind. It was unnerving because I also knew that no one could have entered the building unseen.

One morning I went in, closed the front door, dashed to the alarm, and disengaged it, as usual. I turned around and faced a man who had been standing behind me. I screamed, even though I knew no one could hear me, and he disappeared into thin air. I ran out to the car and tried to bring the dog in, but she would not cross the threshold. I waited to reenter until an employee arrived. In the meantime I pretended that I was watering the herb garden.

That night while we were having dinner I told the family what had happened. Then the girls opened up and told us that someone walked in the hallway every night and that is why they had kept asking their father whether he had been working in his office the night before.

My husband then related how he was locking his office door one evening after the shops were closed and had seen a man walk upstairs, pass him, and go through the locked door of one of the shops (my old office). He also said that things in his office were moved around constantly even though no one had been in the room. The description of the man matched the man that I had encountered that morning.

The next morning I called all of my staff together and told them what had been transpiring. Several of the girls told me about a woman who appeared in the bathroom. She just sat and watched them and then disappeared through the locked door. This had been happening for some time, but they didn't even mention it to one another because it seemed so weird.

One employee had been pushed down the outside back stairs as she carried bags of groceries for the restaurant. I myself was pushed out of the greenhouse, holding an armful of flowers, and fell to the ground. I was the only one there, yet I could feel someone pushing me.

The motion detector went off so frequently that we had it disconnected. The police dispatcher would call us at two or three in the morning and tell us that the ghosts were walking. One of us would rush down, let the officers in, and then listen as the footsteps went upstairs. All of the shops were opened, checked, and, as usual, there was no sign of anyone.

The long hallway upstairs was lined with paintings and prints of women. One morning as an officer was leaving, something hit him in the leg. Dick turned on the light to check it out. A painting of a girl that had hung about twenty-five feet away had flown off the wall and hit him. The picture hook was still in the wall and the wire on the back of the painting was intact. He was shaken and said, "I hope I never get a call to this place again!"

Finally I had had enough of all of this and decided to sell the building. Then all hell broke loose. Doors were pulled off the hinges and tossed down the hall. Merchandise fell off storage shelves, just missing my head, while I was packing. Eggs bounced out of cartons on the counter and broke on the floor—a dozen at a time, while several of us watched in disbelief.

We later sold the building and I closed the restaurant. Eventually the new owners leased out the restaurant. Our younger daughter was in having lunch when the owner came to her table and asked whether the building was haunted. While my daughter was deciding on an answer, the owner watched her and gleefully cried, "I knew it! I knew it! Every night about 9:30 p.m. I hear someone walking upstairs, and I know there is no one there!" She loved ghosts.

Later I asked the fellow who had operated the gallery before us whether he had ever felt any presence. He stated that a man sat on his bed every night at bedtime and then disappeared, never causing any trouble.

I questioned a later restaurant operator, and he told me that all the while they were remodeling downstairs rooms, nails popped back out of the new beams as fast as the carpenters nailed them in. The carpenters' ladders were moved constantly, when unattended, to the other side of the room.

Things always happened so quickly, and we were so entranced that we never taped or photographed anything. But chills ran up and down our spines so frequently that we became believers.

To our knowledge, no one has died in the building or been killed. We like to think the "people" we saw were dissatisfied customer of the bordello before our time.

A ROOM WITH SOMETHING EXTRA

LISA D. GRAZIANO

Suddenly I was awake, wide awake, with the feeling that my husband and I weren't alone in the room. I sat up and listened hard for any sounds of movement. The room was pitch black, and I was terrified to move or even breathe.

Gradually my eyes began to perceive some of the basic shapes within the room. There were the windows opposite me and to the left of the bed, and large fernlike plants hanging in the corners. There was the chaise lounge in the right corner and, to the right, the door to the hall.

My impulse was to bolt for the door, but I was too paralyzed with fear to even twitch. I listened as hard as I could and tried to blink away the darkness—then I heard the sound that gave me chills. It was the floorboards creaking, as if someone were walking slowly across the room just beyond the foot of the bed, in the direction of the windows on the left of the room. In one quick movement I flicked on the light. No one was there. Just me, and my sleeping husband, who was annoyingly unperturbed.

I still had this uncanny feeling that we weren't alone. My heart was pounding in my chest, and I tried to calm myself. I ordered myself to breathe deeply and slowly. Think. Nothing about the room looked unusual; everything was in its proper place. I directed my attention toward the windows. Maybe one was ajar, but they looked secure. In fact everything looked exactly as it had when we went to bed. I glanced over at the clock, 3:20 a.m. Then I remembered that someone had told me that hauntings generally occurred about 3:00 a.m. Oh great, I thought. What I'm listening for may not even be of this world. I couldn't decide what was more terrifying—the prospect of some unknown supernatural being sharing my room or that of some deranged human prowling around.

It had been ten or fifteen minutes since I had heard any discernible sounds, and finally I began to relax a little. I started to rationalize that I had just imagined those sounds. I've always had an overactive imagination. I looked at the clock again—nearly 4:00 a.m. I really had to try to go back to sleep, I thought. Turning off the lights was out of the question, of course, so I settled back against the pillows and tried to doze off. Just as I was beginning to feel my muscles loosen, I felt it—the distinct sensation of a hand lightly passing across my outstretched leg. Instantly I recoiled and sat bolt upright, my eyes widening farther than I thought possible and my heart racing all over again. Now this I was sure I hadn't imagined.

Not willing to keep my fear to myself, I shook my husband awake. I filled him in on current events and groggily he sat up and looked around the room with me. He heard the creaking, but we both agreed that it could be attributed to the wood floors and the place settling. Neither of us had the nerve to actually get out of bed though. Then his eyes widened, and he grabbed my arm and said, "Look!"

I followed his gaze but didn't see anything at first. "What is it?" I asked cautiously. "Can't you see it? On the closet door," he said. I stared at the door in disbelief, unable to say anything. On the door was the faint but discernible silhouette of a woman in an old-fashioned dress with an apron, her hair fastened up in a bun. We didn't move for what seemed the longest time, but finally the image faded away. By the time we got back to sleep it was nearly dawn.

What was it we encountered that night? Was there really some being in the room with us? We might never know. Ultimately we found out that the house had been built in the 1920s, and that the room we were occupying had connected to the next room, which was originally a nursery. Maybe a nanny from the past was trying to get us to let her into the nursery, the entrance to which was now walled up. We certainly didn't expect such an occurrence in the midst of a large city, but to this day we both get goose bumps just thinking about that night.

THE TALL MAN IN THE DOORWAY

BETTY S. ENGLISH

My home was built in the 1800s, and, like many houses of the time, is a "four on four," with a wide hallway down the middle and a twenty-one-step stairway going to the second floor. Other rooms were later added to the back.

In the early 1940s, the couple who lived there very much wanted to have a family and fill this big house with the happy sounds of children. Unfortunately this did not happen, and the house remained quiet and dark. The man died and his widow lived on there for some years.

When my husband and I were looking for more space for ourselves and our five children, we thought this house was perfect. We bought it and began to paint, clean, open windows, and replace light bulbs. We filled it with children and old family furniture, including a bed that was more than one hundred years old.

The house took on a happy glow as music and laughter came from all around. But before long we began to hear other sounds—doors opening and closing, and footsteps, especially in the kitchen and on the stairs.

My husband worked nights, and the children and I were often in the house alone. One night we were all in bed. One lamp had been left on in the den for my husband, and it made a soft light in the hallway.

After sleeping for a time, I awoke and turned toward the bedroom door. There, silhouetted in the door, was the figure of a man. He was quite tall and seemed to be watching over me. He was dressed in a long overcoat and wore a wide-brimmed hat that was pulled down, covering part of his face. I closed my eyes and thought, "What a vivid dream I'm having!" I never felt afraid or threatened but rather cared for, and I believed that someone was glad we were there. I never mentioned this to anyone.

Some weeks later on a Saturday morning, our son Mark, who was ten at the time, said, "Mother, who came to see us last night?"

"No one, why?"

"Did Granddaddy come by?"

"No, Mark, you know he's in Florida. Why?"

"Mother, someone was here last night! I saw him."

"Oh, you probably saw Daddy."

"No, Dad was in his chair asleep; I could hear him snoring!"

"Tell me just exactly what happened."

"Well, something woke me up. I got up and walked out in the hall and looked over the banister railing into the downstairs hall. There was a man standing looking into your bedroom. Then he walked down the hall and went into the study."

"What did he look like?"

"That was the funny part. He was real tall and looked like someone out of an old-time movie. He had on a long overcoat—and a big hat."

That was twenty years ago. My children have grown, married, and moved away. But I still sleep in that more-than-century-old bed, and I now live in that house all alone. *Or do I?*

THE DECOY

PATRICIA VAN EPPS

I had a wonderful uncle who died about fifteen years ago. His hobby was carving wooden fish decoys, and his masterful carvings have, incidentally, now gained him a certain amount of national acclaim. I have had one of those decoys hanging on a wall in my home for many years, securely wired to a screw in the wall.

One day I was inexplicably overcome with memories of my uncle— the wonderful times I had with him, all the kindness he showed me. I was so overwhelmed with these thoughts—unlike anything I had ever experienced—that I had to sit down. As I sat reminiscing, I heard the sound of something crashing to the floor. When I went into the hall to investigate, I found the fish decoy that my uncle had carved lying on the floor.

THE MINERS OF FRENCH GULCH

LYNETTE DADDOW

We still get goose bumps when we recall this incident, even though it happened eight years ago.

Stomp. Stomp. Stomp.

My husband Dennis sat straight up inside his sleeping bag. Stomp. Stomp. The heavy footsteps came closer and then stopped. Two angry voices mumbled at each other, but they were too far away for him to distinguish the words.

Dennis slipped his hand over my mouth to keep me from shouting and shook me to wake me up. He whispered "Listen!" into my ear. The alarm in his voice sent a chill down my spine.

Stomp. Stomp. Stomp. Now the footsteps seemed to be less than ten feet from the tent.

". . . get the guns from the . . ."

". . . show them who's boss around here . . ."

Dennis picked up the flashlight and slithered to the tent door. I grabbed his arm, barely breathing. "Don't go!" I said, panic rising in my throat. "Have to," he murmured.

He carefully unzipped the tent door. Then in one swift motion he stood, directed the flashlight toward the voices, and turned on the light. Nothing.

Dennis whispered, "Let's sit in the Jeep." It seemed more secure to have metal and glass surrounding us instead of the flimsy nylon tent. We cracked the windows to listen. We waited, holding our breaths.

Stomp, stomp, stomp, stomp, stomp.

We heard dozens of heavy footfalls, as if men were passing alongside the Jeep and marching on down the gravel road toward the ghost town of Lincoln. Dennis quickly turned on the headlights. Again nothing.

Needless to say, we spent an uneasy, sleepless night sitting in the Jeep. In the morning, there were no traces of footsteps on the gravel road.

The French Gulch area in Colorado was the site of violent fights between management and miners around the turn of the century. A number of miners were killed in the fighting. We reckon that the residue of rage and wrath in that canyon lingers on.

Other members of our family have also had experiences with the ghosts of French Gulch. My brother and his family were sitting in a heavy canvas army tent one drizzly evening with a Coleman lantern for light. A sharp gust of wind blew inside (and only inside) the tent and extinguished the lantern, despite the glass globe protecting the flame. (That tent is so heavy, the wind can't blow through it.)

My parents also used to camp quite often in that canyon because of its beauty and interesting history. They heard the stomping footfalls on many occasions.

Now none of us spends the night there unless we go camping in a group—good old safety in numbers. Laughter and singing around the campfire seem to ward off the spirits of the angry gold miners.

LADY IN LACE

CLAUDIA HARTFORD

I grew up in Salem, Massachusetts, where there is no lack of ghosts. About one-and-a-half years after I married my first husband, we purchased a home that was built in the year 1801. My husband and I were young and full of excitement and enthusiasm—our house was a large dilapidated one that we were going to restore. I was also eight months pregnant with our first child.

My husband moved into the house while I was hospitalized to have our baby. Two weeks later, daughter Erin and I came home to our new house, which I slept in that evening for the first time. Some evenings when I would go into the kitchen to heat the late-night feeding bottles, I could sense a pair of eyes watching me. I felt a chill in the air and could smell an odor of sweet flowers, almost like honeysuckle, and there was no honeysuckle around!

As my husband went about renovating the house—constantly knocking down walls, sawing, and hammering—we both sensed we had disturbed someone or something. Many nights we were awakened by the sound of glass shattering; when we tiptoed out of the bedroom to investigate, no glass was ever found.

We knew we had a ghost in the house. Later we learned that the house had been a lace factory in the early 1800s and had then been converted into a barn. Several times in the next couple of years we would enter our daughter's bedroom and see her talking and pointing to someone in her closet. One night I saw a figure—no face, but a shadowy body—dressed all in white lace.

In June 1979 we sold our home and moved west. Six years later, while back east visiting, we ran into the home's present owner, who immediately invited us to stop by. As we were all sitting in the living room talking, I asked whether they had met our "friend." She answered, "Oh, you mean the ghost!" We were astonished, and she explained how she and her husband had had several encounters with her.

To this day I imagine the lady in the lace dress still visits the old New England homestead.

THE SATURDAY NIGHT GHOST

DOUGLAS BURGER

In 1974 I was twenty-one years old. I had been living in a small flat when a friend, Dave, suggested we rent a house together. After a couple of weeks of looking, we found a charming old house in Upland, California. Most of the homes in the area were about ninety years old at the time, and this one was no exception. Old houses have always been favorites of mine because they often have more charm than newer houses do. This house had a big front porch, hardwood floors, and a formal dining room with a built-in china hutch—it was a great find, we thought.

The day Dave and I moved in was a Saturday, and we worked all day hauling boxes, moving furniture, setting up beds, and doing all those other tiring tasks that make moving such a delightful experience. By about 9:00 p.m. we had accomplished the larger part of the move and were both so exhausted we decided to call it quits, take showers, and go to bed.

I had the front bedroom, which opened into the living room by way of French doors. Dave's bedroom was off the dining room and was directly behind mine. The two rooms were joined by a shared walk-in closet. I had been in bed about fifteen minutes and was starting to drift off to sleep when I heard what sounded like muffled conversation coming from the living room. The voices sounded young, and I thought perhaps some friends had dropped by to see our new place, found that we had gone to bed, and let themselves in to leave a note. Grudgingly I got out of bed, put on some pants, and went out to say hello.

As I opened the doors to the living room, the voices abruptly stopped. I was quite surprised to find the room empty. Not really knowing what to think, but supposing I might have actually already been asleep and dreaming, I muttered a bit and returned to bed.

Some five to ten minutes later I heard the voices again. This time I was sure I was awake. I was about to get up to investigate once more when I heard Dave open the door to his room and walk into the dining room, which adjoined the living room. Once again the voices abruptly stopped. I got out of bed and walked into the living room to find Dave standing there in his pajamas looking mighty perplexed. He related that he had heard the voices on both occasions as well and had in fact heard me get up to investigate and had noted the voices stopping as I opened the door to my room.

We discussed various theories about the origin of the voices, deciding that perhaps they were from a neighbor's television or something. Frankly, we were too tired to spend much energy worrying over what we might have heard. We went back to bed and promptly fell asleep. The incident was then forgotten.

About three weeks after we moved in, I got up on a Sunday morning and walked into the dining room, heading for the kitchen. I noted that there were three places set for breakfast. Entering the kitchen, I found Dave busily preparing eggs, bacon, and hash browns. I inquired as to who our guest was.

"Isn't Melissa here?" Dave asked. Melissa and I had been dating for six months or so.

"No," I replied, "what makes you think she is?"

"Last night I got up to go to the bathroom and as I walked through the dining room I could swear I saw her going into your room. I'm positive I saw a gal with long blond hair walk into your room," Dave said.

"I should be so lucky. You're seeing things, Dave," was my answer to that. We let it drop and didn't discuss the occurrence again until later on when it was brought forcibly back to mind.

About a week later we were thoroughly settled and decided we should have a housewarming party. Once again it was a Saturday night. Guests began arriving about 8:00 p.m. and by 9:00 some twenty people were mingling, having already received the ten-cent tour. I was in the kitchen preparing snacks when my friend Jim called to me from the living room, "Melissa's here." I was quite surprised because Melissa was working that evening as far as I knew, and I wasn't expecting her to attend. Walking out to the living room I asked Jim where she was. Jim, who was headed over to open the front door, swore that he'd seen her looking in the window on the porch. He opened the door, stuck his head out, and then turned to me, looking confused. "Nobody's there," he said.

"Okay, fine," I said as I returned to the kitchen. About an hour later, my friend Stuart, who had just arrived and had therefore missed Jim's run-in with a Melissa look-alike, had an identical experience. He swore he'd seen Melissa looking in the window. "If it wasn't Melissa, it was a young lady with long blond hair anyway," said Stuart.

By this time the subject of ghosts had been broached. All the episodes experienced in the house were thoroughly discussed, with Dave voicing the opinion that the house was haunted and me stating unequivocally that I didn't believe in such nonsense. As we discussed the topic, I pulled a chair in from the dining room and was sitting in the living room with perhaps ten of our guests. In the midst of the discussion I said, "All right, ghost or ghosts—if there is such a thing—I've had it; quit messing around and come on out and show yourself!" No sooner had the words left my mouth than I found myself sitting on the floor. The chair had been pulled out from under me!

I promptly apologized to the ghost, and, believe me, I was shaking. After my comeuppance at the party, the ghost was not seen or heard from again. We moved out of the house some six months later because I was moving to northern California. The house was demolished a few years back to make room for a parking lot. I can assure you though, I'll never forget my close encounter with a young, willful, blond ghost with a penchant for Saturday nights.

PHANTOM HOOFBEATS

RICHARD J. ZIKA

Where is the boundary line drawn between the natural and the supernatural, or between fact and fantasy? Is a sharp delineation always possible?

It was April 1944 and our company, Casual Dog Detachment, U.S. Army K-9 Corps, was on its way to its first overseas stop, Kanchrapara, a debarkation area approximately thirty-five miles northeast of Calcutta, India.

Our camp itself was situated roughly a mile and a half east of the main north-south road and was reached by a dirt track that had been hacked through jungle growth. The track was adequate enough for military vehicle traffic, but the luxuriant foliage canopy above it prevented much sunlight from reaching it, much less the feeble rays of the moon at night.

Along this track, about one-quarter mile west of our assigned space, lay the ruins of an ancient temple, a foreboding jumble of fallen stones and crumbling masonry ensnared by vegetation, inhabited now only by the inevitable snakes and the large black lizards of the region.

Our tent area lay to the north of this track in a clearing roughly fifty yards wide, hemmed in on two sides by dense jungle growth. Farther to the north the terrain drifted into scattered rice paddies, alternating with stands of dense scrub.

On the south side of the track was the dog space, situated in a bamboo grove cleared enough to permit light and air to get in but sufficiently thick to block out the blistering rays of the tropical sun.

It was our second night ashore and I, along with another member of our company, had drawn the 2400 to 0600 guard duty. Two men, each with a trained dog, were certainly sufficient to watch over our small encampment of 100 dogs and 108 people. My post was the front half of the camp, and on my rounds I could check the dirt track and peer into the mottled shadows of the dog area.

The night could only be described as something out of Kipling. From the nearest village drifted the sounds of tunes in a minor key played by lutes, high-pitched pipes, and muted drums and cymbals, giving proof to the adage that "India is the land that never sleeps." The moon was the stuff of legends, so full and bright you could count every blade of grass. My dog's coat gleamed with burnished shades of black and tan, and the white-capped tents took on the aspect of gigantic toadstools.

Yet, in the jungle, the night was absolutely black, impenetrable to the eye of either man or dog. From its lightless womb uncountable species of insects added their nightly symphony to the stars to the never-ending howls of the jackals and the occasional cursing of a monkey disturbed in its sleep.

Abruptly, as though directed by the wave of a conductor's baton, the night noises in the direction of the temple ceased and, simultaneously, my dog alerted with a low, menacing, belly-deep growl, his hackles rising to the perpendicular. Then the whole dog area became strangely restive, with growls, whimpers, snuffling, and much movement.

Then I heard it—the unmistakable sound of an unshod horse galloping along the dirt track. Coming from the direction of the temple ruins, it was approaching fast. Just as fast, I unslung my carbine and strained my eyes, trying to see into the inky black. Nothing could be seen. My own hackles began rising under my helmet as I prepared to challenge. Closer and closer came the pounding hooves until, abruptly, the sound broke into the revealing light of the moon. *Nothing!*

I couldn't sound an alarm: there was nothing there. Yet the hoof-beats passed within a few feet of me on my right, causing my dog to alternately snarl and lunge, pulling against his leash. At the same time I felt a rush of air—not cool, but cold and clammy air.

As abruptly as it began the incident ended. The hoofbeats were cut off as though in midstride and, shortly thereafter, one by one, the night noises resumed. To say I was unnerved would be an understatement, but what was I to do? Sound an alarm about being run down by nothing and become the laughingstock of the camp? No, this had to be thought out carefully and played the same way.

When next our rounds crossed I asked my sentry partner whether he'd noticed anything unusual. Oh, sure. He had noticed the unrest in the dog area; as a matter of fact, his own dog had briefly alerted. But he himself had seen or heard nothing.

He peered into my face. "Hey, what's the matter, Zeke?" he asked. "How come you look so pale? D'ja see a ghost or something?"

I could only manage a weak smile and shake my head. There are times when it's best to keep one's mouth shut.

Much as I tried, I couldn't help but wrestle with the matter over and over in my mind. Was it only a case of jitters? Did the full, tropical moon and the strangeness of it all play tricks on my mind? Many, I was sure, would think this. Maybe I should accept it myself.

But, if this were true, why did two fully trained dogs come to alert? And why did ninety-eight other trained dogs pay witness to their alert? And last, but far from least, what was that clammy cold of the grave that had rushed past me?

Three days later, while I was still trying to convince myself that the incident hadn't—couldn't have—happened, I came across information that gave me a chilling pause for thought.

Natives of the region shunned the temple ruins. Local legend had it that in its day the temple had been the scene of bizarre and violent happenings. It was still thought to be a place of evil, complete with strange apparitions and manifestations.

Ignorant superstition you say? Perhaps. In turn I must ask again: Where is that nebulous boundary line that marks where the natural leaves off and the supernatural begins?

"I'LL BE BACK"

RICHARD ROTHROCK

In 1989 I lived in a one-bedroom apartment that occupied the second floor of a two-story house. One night shortly after moving in I awoke to the sound of someone walking down the hallway outside my bedroom. At first I thought it was my cat. The hallway's old wooden floor creaked loudly regardless of the weight of the walker. But then I saw my cat asleep next to me. I noticed that the footsteps came not from my living room, but from the other direction, which dead-ended at my bathroom.

Before I could think more about it, a tall, slender man walked into the room. He paused in front of my bookcase and stared at me. He wore a blue windbreaker and a red baseball cap and looked to be in his early sixties. He just stared. I wondered whether this was only my imagination, but a quick glance at my cat revealed that he was staring at the visitor, too. I turned my attention back to the man.

"Can I help you?" I asked.

The man shook his head. "No. I was just looking around. I'll be back later to talk."

Without another word, he walked out of the room and back down the hall. When the footsteps reached the bathroom, they stopped. I pondered checking the bathroom but decided against it.

The next day I called a friend who had lived in the apartment before I moved in. I asked whether anything strange had occurred while she lived here.

"Blue windbreaker? Red baseball cap?" she asked.

I laughed.

She said he came into the bedroom one night shortly after she moved in. He told her he would be back but never returned.

MOVING IN

JAN AGUILAR

In July 1978 we moved our family from Colorado to California, and since we had lived in the Bay Area before our move to Colorado, we were anticipating getting back home.

We found a unique, secluded home on nearly an acre of land. The house had been built in 1962, and the architect had used some natural redwood paneling and doors that had been taken from a summer cabin built on the property in the 1930s. The property had long stayed in the family of the original owner, and we were the first new owners.

One day soon after we moved in I decided it was time to stock the kitchen. My husband and son were gone for the day, so my daughter and I did the shopping and returned to the house about forty-five minutes later.

After washing the lettuce, I turned on the garbage disposal; there was a terrible clunk-clunk sound and then a jam. I reached my hand down and felt a large metal object—it was an old, rusted pocketknife. It broke the garbage disposal, of course, and when my husband and son returned that evening, I asked them whether they had ever seen the knife before.

They answered no and we all wondered where it could have come from; before I left to shop I had meticulously scoured the kitchen sink and had run the disposal. It had worked perfectly.

The following Saturday my husband's business partner from Los Angeles came to spend the weekend. In the early evening we were sitting on a patio off the kitchen when old college friends dropped in. When the weather turned a little cool, we all went inside. About ten minutes later, all five of us heard a tremendous shattering of glass in the kitchen area. We all jumped up and ran to the kitchen and patio, checking everywhere. Nothing could be found—not one shard of glass!

After our friends left, my husband and I were determined either to find the broken glass or to move out. We finally gave up at 2:00 a.m. after searching every inch of every cupboard and drawer and scouring the patio for the broken glass. We were exhausted, but we did stay.

Our friends never visited us again in the evening. Before retiring, the business partner said, "Maybe I'm not your only houseguest. Maybe you have a ghost!"

Our roof needed repair work, and we soon became familiar with the sounds of footsteps and hammering on the roof. We were also familiar with the noises of birds that went skittering across it, and the thumping of an occasional squirrel or raccoon.

Shortly after the shattered-glass experience, we were awakened early one Sunday morning to the sound of heavy footsteps and hammering on our roof. My first thought was "I'd better get dressed. What are they doing here on Sunday?" My husband got up and looked out our windows expecting to see a truck in our driveway. There was no truck and no crew and the noises quickly stopped. Once again, we seriously thought of "getting rid of this house and its resident ghost!" But I had made arrangements to have new carpeting installed in a few days, and we were expecting company from Colorado.

The focal point of our living room is a large, very heavy, antique pewter chandelier that was in the house when we bought it. Right after the carpet installers left, the chandelier started swaying in a circular motion and, believe me, nothing less than a good-sized earthquake could move *that* chandelier! By this time I was starting to become accustomed to the idea that we had a ghost.

I stood back from the swaying chandelier and said in a loud voice, "I'm glad you like the new carpets—I hope you'll like the skylight we're going to put in the kitchen!" The chandelier *stopped* swaying just as suddenly as it had started.

Everything was quiet and normal after that—no more "ghost" occurrences until Christmas Eve, the first in our new home. It was close to

9:00 p.m. Our family gathered around the tree and fireplace, listening to Christmas carols, each of us trying to decide which gift we would choose to open this night.

We weren't expecting company, and it's a long walk up our private drive to the front door. We all heard the footsteps approaching our front door and our two dogs went crazy barking and jumping at the door. We were surprised that someone would come unannounced on Christmas Eve. We waited for the doorbell to ring. It didn't. We got the dogs under control and opened the door, fully expecting someone to be there. There wasn't anyone visible, and my husband and son went way down to the road looking for whoever it was who had come to our door.

I just had to smile and in a loud voice I said, "Thanks for stopping by—and a Merry Christmas to you, too!" Our Christmas tree lights dimmed and then came on very bright.

Maybe it was just a power surge—but most probably it wasn't!

After the first of the year and in subsequent years, a few unexplained things have happened—sprinklers have mysteriously turned on, thermostats have somehow turned themselves up—but I truly believe that our ghost is now happy and satisfied with the new family that occupies his old haunts.

A CLOSET PARTIER

DEBBY SUE VAN DE VENDER

Before I was married I lived in a studio apartment. Following our wedding, my husband moved in. It didn't take long for us to discover that there just wasn't enough room for two adults and a large dog in a New York studio apartment. Because we liked the building, we decided not to move out but to wait for a larger unit.

The agent soon notified us that a one-bedroom in the same building had suddenly become available. My husband could not believe the poor condition of the apartment, but I could see how it could be quite nice with ten to twelve weeks' worth of work. We decided to take it.

We met the new neighbors and explained that there would probably be a bit of noise during the next few months while the painters, plasterers, and floor finishers did their work. It actually took five months before the place was ready. No one raised an objection; in fact, everyone was quite understanding.

Almost every day when we returned from work we ate dinner and then went upstairs to see our new home.

The first evening I went up alone and stood in the middle of the living room, smiling happily. I noticed that sounds reverberated in the empty apartment. I didn't think much of the laughter I heard coming from next door. Actually, I was pleased to know that we had cheerful neighbors. I mentioned it to my husband when he came home, and he agreed that it was a good omen.

A few days later, I met one of our new neighbors. She asked how we liked living upstairs. I explained that the work had not yet been completed and that we were still living downstairs. She winked and said, "Oh, I understand how it is with young people. You know I was young once myself. But it is nice that you are enjoying the bedroom."

A few weeks later another neighbor stopped to ask how we were doing in our new home. Again I explained that we would not be moving in for another two months. "Isn't that strange?" said the neighbor. "I thought I heard you giggling the other night."

Our downstairs neighbor began to complain about the "dancing" he heard at night and in the early morning. "When are you getting your rugs?" was his constant inquiry. I explained, again, that we had not yet moved. He wrote letters to the management office complaining of the noise. The agent, however, knew that we were still living downstairs and explained the situation to the neighbor. He did not retreat. He continued to complain about "night noises."

My husband, upon hearing these stories, simply said that the sounds the neighbors were hearing came from other apartments and were resonating through our empty new home.

We finally did make the move. We took time off from our jobs so that we could get settled as quickly as possible. The kitchen cabinets were lined and filled. The phones, the television cable, and the rugs arrived the next morning. We busied ourselves with hanging clothing in the closets, storing dishes, and introducing our dog to her new surroundings.

Each time my husband or I put something in my bedroom closet we would leave the door open, only to return with another armful of stuff to find the closet door closed. That wasn't a problem—we thought there must be something wrong with the spring, the bolt, the door, or something.

I took an extra day off so I could go marketing and have dinner on the table when my husband arrived for our first night in our new home. Everything was perfect.

At about two o'clock in the morning, our dog awakened me. I thought, "Oh great, she's in a new place and she's nervous and needs a walk." As I got up to dress I heard the sound of giggling. I woke my husband to tell him I was going out with the dog, but then I saw that she had curled up and gone back to sleep. I hadn't taken that long to dress, and when she asks it's always because she really needs to go out.

While she slept, my husband and I tried to figure out where the giggling was coming from. It seemed to be from the inside of one of our bedroom closets. The laughter got louder as we approached the closet but stopped suddenly when we opened the door.

Fortunately, the laughter is not a nightly occurrence. One of our friends explained that our visitor is happy to have us and means us no harm, although she (her sex having been determined by the fact that it is my clothing that gets moved and my closet that is invaded) can be mischievous and playful. We don't know why she is here, but as long as she is polite and relatively quiet she is welcome to stay.

After several weeks, we began to refer to her as Priscilla, and now, when something falls in the night or there is a strange sound, we just explain to our guests that Priscilla is probably getting ready for a date. She has never destroyed anything. Even our dog has adjusted to having "someone" else in our home and no longer growls at Priscilla.

At this point, Priscilla is part of our family. Should we ever move, I hope she will come with us.

GOODNIGHT KISSES

KEN LEPPER

It was a dark and stormy night—well, not actually, but I've always wanted to start a story that way.

"Good night!" we all said with various smiles and whispers as Papa (my grandfather) turned out the lights. We were all in a large, rectangular room, built years before any of us were born. There were cots and beds lined up military style down two walls. The only doorway led into the kitchen.

It was the Christmas season of 1956 and my sister and I, along with our parents, had traveled from Phoenix to Hayward, California, to visit my grandparents, aunts, uncles, and cousins. In a few days we would open presents and eat a magnificent Italian Christmas dinner. We were all very excited, and trying to fall asleep was neither a quiet nor a calm exercise.

One by one, we all felt drowsiness overcome exuberance. The darkness in the room painted everything in barely discernible but soft shapes and shades of gray. We all felt safe. We were surrounded by family and generations of love.

As we began to fall asleep, someone could be heard entering the room. Drowsy and comfortable, I didn't even open my eyes but could hear breathing and the rustle of clothing as someone bent over my cousin Jonathan, whose cot was next to the doorway. I heard what sounded like a murmur and a kiss and then felt the presence bend over me as well. There was cautious movement and breathing above me. Even with my eyes closed, I knew that someone was just above my face, looking at me as parents do when they at last have an opportunity to watch us in slow motion.

I smelled tobacco, just as on my father's breath, and assumed it was he. I felt a light kiss, and then snuggled into my pillows. He moved around my bed and over to my sister, who was deeper into the room, lying in the next bed.

Again I sensed him, this time bending over my sister. She timidly questioned, "Daddy?" There was no answer, though my sister could obviously sense his presence. She called out more loudly, "Daddy!" Still no answer.

He didn't move, nor did he answer. Something in my sister's voice awakened my cousins, who began to ask who was there.

Jonathan sat up and turned on the light.

No one was there! No one stood next to my sister. No one could have left the room. There was only one way out, past Jonathan and me, and none of us had sensed or seen anyone leaving.

Instantly the room went from warmth to terror. Several of the children became hysterical. My sister wailed the loudest. Parents came scrambling downstairs, fearing the worst.

We were calmed and hugged and kissed and held until we all stopped shouting or crying. We were assured that it must have been our imagination. A light was left on in the kitchen to help us feel safer. Hours later, we finally accepted our parents' words and fell asleep.

As children, we never wondered why our parents did not accuse us of telling stories or of trying to scare each other. Years later my mother told me that, when she was a girl in the house, members of the family would often see the outline of a man in the kitchen doorway. It was always at night. He would just stand there, and if one walked toward him, he would either fade away or turn around and walk into the same room where we had been sleeping.

Perhaps his grave was under the room, my mother suggested. Or perhaps he had died while building the home. No one knew, and, for all we know, he could still be there today.

I do know, however, that we were not threatened that night. We were safe. We were loved by a spirit that in the anonymity that darkness offers simply sought to comfort us and wish us sweet dreams.

LOVE THAT CANNOT DIE

FATHERS

JEANINE MATTISON

When I became pregnant with my first child, my father-in-law was ecstatic. My husband was the last of his seven children to marry and give him grandchildren. He could hardly wait for this child, who was due in late July.

Unfortunately, my father-in-law did not live long enough to witness the happy event. He passed away three months before our son was born in August of 1969.

Because we lived in a large, old, drafty farmhouse, we closed the upstairs for the winter. The baby was in his own room just off the dining room, and my husband and I slept in the living room on a sofa bed.

Late in October I awoke suddenly in the middle of the night for no apparent reason. As I sat up in bed, I saw smoke in the doorway. It was just a tall, thin pillar of smoke. (My father-in-law was more than six feet tall.) At first I was quite alarmed because I suspected a fire. Almost as quickly as I panicked, however, I felt a strange calm come over me and absolutely no need to move or check the baby.

The "smoke" lingered in the doorway momentarily, and then actually turned and went into the baby's room. After a few seconds, the "smoke" left our son's room and came to the foot of our bed, where it remained for a few seconds. It then moved to my husband's side, bent over his head as if to kiss his cheek, and finally dissipated.

I woke my husband and very excitedly explained that his father had just visited us and told him what I had seen. He, of course, thought I was totally nuts.

Two years later we had our second child, a baby girl. My son, who was then repeating everything he heard, was making me crazy one day, saying "Hi, Gus" over and over again. When my husband came home, our son ran to the door yelling "Hi, Gus." My husband's face went white and he asked, "Where did he get that from?" I said we hadn't been out of the house all day and I had no idea, but it was driving me nuts. By then the child had said it at least a thousand times.

My husband said, "Maybe my father *has* visited us. He used to call me that when I was little, and no one else ever did." I had never heard this story before, but I wasn't surprised.

Several years later my husband and I had divorced, and my children and I were living in Florida. My sixteen-year-old sister baby-sat for me while I worked a couple of hours at night at the local credit bureau. One night when I arrived home, she was still up, and she claimed that she would never sleep in my house again unless I was home.

It seemed that she had seen a ghost enter each child's bedroom. She didn't feel threatened or frightened in any way, but she was startled just the same. From the description she gave me of the ghost, I am positive it was my father-in-law again. In fact, I'm sure he made periodic visits to our house for the entire time my children lived with me. They are now twenty and twenty-two years old and, as far as I know, he no longer visits my house. I miss him.

Eight years ago I had a visit from my own father, who died in 1981. While standing at the kitchen sink washing dishes after dinner, I felt hands on my shoulders. Thinking it was my new husband, I turned but found no one there. When I went back to the dishes, I felt the hands again. Dad had done that occasionally when I did dishes at home. This time I stood still and enjoyed the feeling.

That was the only visit I've had from my dad that I'm aware of, although three years ago our rocking chair began to rock by itself.

When I looked at it, it stopped abruptly. As I glanced away, it began to rock again. This happened three times.

Finally I went to the side of the chair, placing my left arm around the back and right arm across the chair arms as if to hug the person in the chair. I said aloud, "Whoever is sitting in my chair, I love you." The chair never rocked again.

OUR YEARS WITH LYDIA

SALLY KURTZMAN

We had been in our new house only a week when I first suspected that something strange was going on.

Starting the second week, I would come downstairs to find all the lights on and the front door wide open. "Come on, Jim," I would urge my husband, "help me out and lock up tightly, please." We had been burglarized in our old house, so I was doubly cautious about locking doors and keeping the house safe. He assured me that he was as concerned as I was and had been locking up and turning off all the lights. No he hadn't, I thought.

Week after week, the same things, as well as new and different things, would happen: doors were open, lights were on, the car parked on the outside landing was on the lower landing, knives were missing, and crockery was broken. We started to sense that perhaps we weren't alone in the house.

A friend of mine has a sister who is a medium, so, in fun, I decided to call her to set up a time for her to come over and perform a séance. My husband warned me, however, that as practicing Catholics we should not do something the Church would be against. So I called the priest who married us, and he said he *was* against séances but that he would be glad to come over and perform an exorcism for us.

"But if you suggest an exorcism, that means you think there's something here," I said. "If there is, why can't I talk with it?" I asked. He couldn't answer that and only urged me not to go ahead with the séance. But I did.

At the first séance, we had quite a bit of activity through something called tabling, during which the table at which the participants are seated knocks and bangs out answers. The table told us that the "something" was named Lydia and that she had lived in the house. There were other people here, too. And yes, it had been Lydia who had opened the doors—to get our attention.

Whoa. For a nice Catholic girl like me, I did find a lot of this tough to believe, but I went along with it. When my husband came home from a basketball game, he was appalled to find me in the middle of this séance. But he stood there enraptured while the table tapped out the score of the basketball game he had just attended and told him who won. He was convinced.

The next day I told my story to a woman who teaches parapsychology. She said that tabling was the easiest of all paranormal tricks and that I had been easily fooled. I began to believe her and was pretty chagrined.

Nevertheless, I did research on the house and found that a woman had died there in a fire and her name *was* Lydia. I found through the abstract of the house that there had been quite a few owners, and I thought that might account for the activity we were having.

A month later we had another séance with the same medium, this time with the parapsychology teacher on hand, plus several friends who couldn't believe all of this. Actually, on the day of the séance there were a dozen or so people who came to our door, having heard from friends of friends that we were doing this. They wanted to know whether they could contact their dead loved ones.

It was like a zoo, with this bunch of people sitting around my table. Soon Lydia was back and answering questions, giving maiden names of people that I didn't know and of whom the medium had no knowledge. The evening was pretty bizarre, and Lydia asked me to contact her daughter.

I ignored the request, feeling that if I contacted anyone that person would think I was crazy. Should I say: "Oh, by the way, your mother would like you to know she's all right"? No, thanks.

We had one last séance six months later, this time with a crew of forty in tow. Some I knew, some I didn't. My sister-in-law had flown in from California and was quite shocked the night before the séance to wake up with what felt like a hair dryer blowing under her nightie. She put her hand against the wall to steady herself and said that she saw an outline of her hand, in what looked like neon light, on the wall. She screamed and woke us up.

That last night we had the usual farfetched questions about relatives, and again we asked Lydia why she was here. We had decided to sell the house, and many people who had looked at it decided that there was some sort of "force field" upstairs (as one Realtor put it) and that this was an unlucky house. Lydia promised that she wasn't thwarting the sale, and she said she wasn't coming with us.

We moved to our new house thirteen years ago, and for a while I would "perform" at parties, telling our new friends ghost stories of lights and phone calls, moved knives (Lydia was very keen on knives), and cars. After a few years, the stories became less frequent because we had been away from the source for some time.

Flash to 1989. I was just out of the shower, a towel around my head, when the doorbell rang. I could see a man and a woman standing there, and I thought they were selling something. I yelled through the door: "What do you want?" They answered that they just wanted to talk to me. I said I wouldn't let them in because I was really busy. They said, "We used to live where you once lived. Our mother died in a fire there."

I opened the door and asked, "Is your mother Lydia?" When they said yes, Margaret (the daughter) and I both started crying.

It had been forty-one years to the day that their mother had been buried. Throughout the years, as children and then as adults, they felt they never had had closure with their mother, so this year Margaret had dragged her brother, Kevin, to town to at least see the old house.

They decided to check each house on all sides of the block to find people who had lived there in 1948. Some of the neighbors remembered my stories, and somehow Margaret and Kevin found out where we lived and called on us.

I told them my stories, everything that we had pieced together: Lydia had died in a fire, had not finished her business on earth, and had not "crossed" over. She wanted to get in touch with her daughter—that was her goal—and somehow sensed that I was a friendly sort, so she tried to get me to help her. Lydia had said that she had tried to use other people in other years.

The daughter and I couldn't talk fast enough. She wasn't as old as I had pictured (she was just forty-seven). I had feared calling some seventy-year-old to say her mother was fine. Later, Margaret sent me clippings all about the fire, and it's amazing that the story pieces somehow fit.

I asked to go to the service they were having so I, too, could get some closure with Lydia, but Margaret said it was personal with her and her brother, so I acquiesced to her wishes. She said that she had felt a great sense of peace throughout the ceremony, and that at the moment the service ended rain burst from the sky, then in a flash stopped. Amazing, she said, adding that it was as if her mother were crying tears of joy.

TWO SMALL WHITE COFFINS

MELINDA SUSAN HILL-MAIER

My grandmother always told this story as absolute fact. She had no doubt that she had somehow received messages three times from the hereafter.

My grandparents, Tom and Goldie Hill, were married in 1910 in Warsaw, Kentucky, and eventually they had six children. In early 1922, Mom Mom had a very disturbing dream in which "someone had pushed two small white coffins up onto the back porch." In October, their fifteen-month-old daughter, Martha Thomas, died of meningitis.

Even though my grandfather was steadily employed, times were hard, and they were "poor as Job's turkey." The local undertaker, who was a friend of the family, knew my grandparents couldn't afford much and kindly donated a tiny white casket for the little girl's funeral.

A few months later, my grandmother again dreamed of the two little white coffins. In August 1923, their four-year-old daughter, Rena, died of diphtheria. Once again the undertaker generously gave them a small white casket.

My grandfather died in 1957 and a son, Sam, passed on a year later. Shortly after Uncle Sam's death, Mom Mom awakened one night and felt her husband standing next to her bed. "It's all right, Goldie," he told her. "Now I have three of the children with me and you have three of them with you." Then Big Daddy departed, never to be heard from again!

Every time Mom Mom got to the part about my grandfather's ghostly visit, I'd ask her if she had been afraid. She would always say, "Why, no sirree! It was only Tom! Why should I be afraid of him?!"

THE MYSTERIOUS RETURN OF MR. FOSTER

SUSAN BOGART NICHOLSON

My husband and I were thrilled when we were given the go-ahead to move into the New England barn-style house with the octagonal roof that we had driven by and loved for months. The house was charming, with high ceilings, lots of mysterious alcoves, and a huge yard. It had had only one previous renter since the owners had passed away there, and we promised the former owners' son that we would treat the house with as much respect as if we owned it personally, which we hoped some day to do.

Shortly after we moved in, we both realized, not telling each other at first, that we were not the only inhabitants—someone else lived there too. We heard footsteps on the stairs at night, smelled bread toasting in the morning, and, during the holidays, heard Christmas carols from an invisible radio. Some nights, when our bedroom door would open and shut, we questioned, did it—or they—come in or go out?

Once, while we were at work, someone tried to force open the front door. The police couldn't understand why the would-be burglar didn't get in, since the easy-access door had been pried open with a knife and a screwdriver. My husband and I both realized that Mrs. Foster had been protecting her home. From then on I never worried about being alone.

One morning while my sister was staying with us and I was already at work, I received a call from her. In a trembling voice she asked me how long I had been at work because she thought I had asked her whether she'd like some toast, and in her sleep she'd mumbled yes. She had smelled the bread toasting, but when she finally wandered downstairs she found an empty kitchen and a cold toaster.

Eventually word of what was happening got back to my landlord's family, and the grandchildren, all adults, came to visit. They were astounded when they found that I had decorated the kitchen in strawberries, as their grandmother had done, and that my newly purchased dining-room set was identical to hers. The list went on.

In the midst of all the warm experiences there was one dark and frightening one. One evening I was hemming a new pair of slacks and, after trimming off the excess and laying them across the bed as I threaded a needle, I picked them back up to find there was blood dripping from each leg. My first reaction was that one of my dogs had had an accident. I put the slacks into cold water and sponged up a salad-plate-sized pool from the hardwood floor. The next day I called the vet and asked whether a virus could have caused one of my dogs to toss up blood and was told it was not possible, given the pure state of the blood. By then the sponge had been rinsed out, but I managed to scrape up some particles of the substance, which I took to the University of California at Davis. They confirmed that it was definitely blood, but they couldn't tell what type. When questioning the Foster relatives again, I was told that Mr. Foster had died in that bedroom and, shortly before his death from emphysema, had hemorrhaged in that very spot. Perhaps my witnessing that event enabled the two Fosters to finally get together, because shortly after that I had my last encounter with them.

I went to bed early that night; my sister had gone to visit some friends. I awoke after midnight to hear laughter and giggling and a man and a woman talking excitedly downstairs. Both of the dogs jumped up and headed downstairs with their tails wagging, but they stopped at the landing. I was annoyed. I thought my sister and her friends were being very rude, and even made several loud comments to that effect. The voices finally stopped, and while I waited for my sister to come upstairs I received a phone call from her telling me that she was going to spend the night with her friends because it had gotten so late. I realized then that I had been a witness to Mr. Foster's return. He had finally come to take his wife, who had been waiting for him for years, away where they could share their eternity. I knew that they would never come back.

I feel privileged that I was able to experience these events. The house was never the same after that; the warmth was gone. It's hard to describe what it was like to sit at the top of the stairs and hear the laughter, listen to the music, and smell the toast, especially when you're talking about ghosts, but I swear that every last word of this account is true.

THE LETTER

MARGARET LOCH

Back in 1981 I decided to plan a special surprise for my mother, who would turn eighty in September 1982. I asked everyone in the family, from the youngest to the oldest, to write her a letter telling her how they felt about her. I also asked her friends from all over the country to write and even managed to get her a note from Tom Selleck, her favorite actor.

I worked for over a year on the project, collecting letters and putting them into a large scrapbook. One night that year, just after going to bed, I felt that someone was in the doorway. I was not asleep and turned my head toward the door. My father, who had been dead for twenty-two years, was standing there. I did not see him clearly but I knew it was him. I was not frightened, for I loved him dearly and knew he meant no harm. I didn't say a word, just lay there looking at him. After a few minutes he walked to the foot of the bed and looked at me. He started to talk softly, and I really had to strain to hear his words.

Finally I understood: my father wanted to add his letter to the book. I reached under my bed for my notebook (I keep one there as I sometimes write poetry in the night), and as he spoke I wrote down what he was saying. When he was done he smiled at me and was gone. I don't know how; he was just gone. I then lay awake for quite a while.

When I woke up the next day I thought maybe I had dreamed the visit, but when I reached under the bed for my notebook, sure enough, there was his letter. I was amazed. He had said, in part, that he would be with my mother—the wife he loved with all his heart—when she cut her birthday cake. He also signed the letter, using an endearment I later learned no one but he and my mother knew.

I agonized for a long time over putting the letter in the book, but I felt that if it had meant enough to him for him to come from wherever he was to dictate it to me, I had to put it in. His letter was the first one in her birthday book.

My father was true to his word. When my mother cut her cake, we took our pictures. When we looked at the pictures after they were developed, we were amazed at the picture of her cutting the cake: over her left shoulder was a white light that was most definitely not a reflection!

GRANDMA'S PIANO

NANCY PALAJAC-SANDERS

I was twenty-six in 1983. The year didn't start out very well. Uncle Tom died in January. My ninety-two-year-old maternal grandmother died on

Valentine's Day. I was getting divorced and waiting to marry John, who is now my husband.

After my grandma, to whom I was very close, died, I grieved deeply and would sit for hours talking to her about my turbulent life. On a romantic level, I believed she could hear me. But realistically I knew that Grandma was dead and gone. I soon found out, however, that though she was dead, she wasn't quite gone.

John moved in with me just before Christmas of 1983. One day, as usual, we got home from work about 5:30 p.m. The sun had disappeared an hour earlier, and John was sitting in the tiny dining room of our apartment lacing up his running shoes. I was in the bedroom changing clothes when I heard his voice.

"I can't hear you, honey. I'm in the bedroom," I called.

"I'm not talking to you, babe. I'm talking to the person standing beside your grandma's piano," he said.

Fear stopped me dead in my tracks. "John, that's not funny. You're scaring me," I answered in a high-pitched voice.

"It's all right, honey," he said. "She's a friendly spirit."

The instant he said "she," I thought of grandma. Pulling my blouse back on, I walked slowly out of the bedroom, turned the corner, and moved into the small kitchen. John was still sitting calmly at the dining room table. "What did you say?" I asked him softly.

"She's gone," John said. "She walked from the piano toward your voice, looking at you. Then she disappeared through you."

I was so flabbergasted that I sat down and asked John to describe the vision: an old woman just under five feet tall, her gray hair pulled into a bun, wearing a white dress with red and blue flowers on it, and a white sweater about her small shoulders.

I didn't know what my brother-in-law, a funeral-home director, had been given to dress Grandma in, so I called Charlie the next day and told him what John had seen. He didn't remember the clothing and advised me to call my mom. He also told me that he has relatives of the deceased telling him similar stories all the time.

I called my mom. She didn't understand why I wondered about Grandma's burial clothes, but she offered the information nevertheless. "It was her favorite dress. The white one with blue and red flowers on it."

I had never told John what my grandma looked like, and he had never seen a picture of her. He hadn't even met any of my family members yet. We had become serious only after my grandma had passed away. My only explanation for this experience is that she came to see whether I was all right.

I had done enough crying and praying that year after she had died to literally raise the dead. I was disappointed that she had appeared to John and not to me, but John had seen spirits before. He thinks she knew I would have been too shocked and afraid to see her.

The baby grand piano that John saw her standing next to was my grandma's. She used to play "The Irish Jig" on it for me all the time.

A year later when we were moving to a new home, two young boys and an old man were charged with hauling the piano up the stairs of our two-story condo. While John and I were in the master bedroom unpacking, the old man and elder boy were down in the garage getting more boxes. The younger boy was asked to set up the piano. Suddenly we heard a frightened gasp, and the young boy called out our names.

We hurried out to the living room and were confronted by the young boy with his back against the wall opposite the piano, screwdriver still gripped tightly in his fist.

"I had the screws on the floor, getting ready to put the legs on," the boy countered when asked to explain. "When I turned back to the piano, the screws were already in and tightened!"

THE DOUGHBOY OF WORLD WAR I

GENELLE TOWNER

Uncle Bill was just seventeen in April 1917 when he joined up as an infantryman (doughboy) in World War I, lying about his age in order to enlist. He left his parents, two brothers, and three sisters behind when he sailed for France.

Aunt Truth—two years older than Bill—taught him to ride a spirited stallion bareback and standing up, played violin next to his clarinet in the family orchestra, and, as a sleepwalker, valued his presence as her protector as she roamed up and down the ancestral hallway in the wee small hours. Bill was the brother who always saw Truth safely back to her own room following these nocturnal wanderings. They were as close as two peas in a pod.

The day after Bill's departure for France from Gold Town, Texas, Truth and Grandma got out the Ouija board and asked: "Is Bill well?" For six months the answer was "Yes." Then one night Grandma and Truth had the same dream: the doorbell rang and when the door was opened, a Western Union messenger thrust a telegram into their hands with the news of Bill's death in France.

The next morning they immediately got out the Ouija board. "Is Bill well?" "No." "Is Bill dead?" "Yes."

One week later, the doorbell really did ring. When Grandma and Truth answered the door, the same unsmiling delivery boy they had seen in their dreams stood before them, visibly shaking as he handed them the death telegram. Grandma and Truth sailed to France to visit Bill's grave and place flowers on it.

One stormy October night in 1937, when I was fourteen, I heard stealthy footsteps going up and down the hallway at Grandma's after midnight. The wind howled as I peeked out the door and saw Truth walking with a handsome World War I doughboy. She was sound asleep, walking with her arms outstretched; the doughboy walked behind, carrying a gleaming clarinet. There was no music, only the wind. I shivered and shook for the remainder of the night, pulling the covers up over my head.

When I asked Grandma about it the next morning, she was not at all concerned. "Just Truth and Bill. It's the anniversary walk. We've learned to expect it every year," she said, and she refused to say more.

For years, on October 31, the anniversary of his death, the Doughboy of World War I walked up and down the ancestral hallway, often joining Truth on her midnight journeys, sometimes silent, sometimes playing "Over There" on his clarinet.

By the year 1967, both Grandma and Grandpa were dead, and the family home had been sold to the local newspaper, the *Gold Town Sen-*

tinel. My grandparents' old house had been moved to another part of town, and the *Gold Town Sentinel* was housed in a brand-new building on the site formerly occupied by my grandparents' home. Truth was well-acquainted with the city editor of the graveyard shift at the newspaper, a former student of hers named Leo Maguire.

Every October 31 from 1967 to 1987, the twenty years that he served as city editor of the *Sentinel*, Leo listened with fear and trepidation in the wee small hours of the morning to the haunting refrain of "Over There" from a clarinet and watched in amazement as a stalwart young doughboy marched solemnly up and down the corridor just outside his office, vanishing in a misty vapor at the last note of the plaintive song.

Leo died in an automobile accident in December 1987, and Truth passed away just before New Year's Day in 1988, when she would have celebrated her ninetieth birthday. No one has seen the doughboy since that date and no one has heard the mournful notes of "Over There" played by the young World War I hero. His days of protecting his sister are over, and his music is of another world.

HUGS FROM MY BROTHER

JILL ROSSETTO

A few years ago my two-year-old daughter Ashley and I stopped by the local cemetery where my dad and brother are buried. Dad had died twenty years before, and my brother Larry was laid to rest ten years later on the other side of the cemetery.

I drive by this graveyard at least three times a week, and I find it comforting to stop in once in a while. This particular day I made my usual visit to both graves and then wandered over to an older section of the graveyard—the older headstones and the history on them have always interested me. My daughter was entertaining herself, following along and climbing on a few of the shorter tombstones, when suddenly she turned around and started running toward my brother's grave. I called to her a couple of times, but she kept running for about twenty yards until she was directly in front of the headstone. She stopped, crouched, and just stared at his marker. When I caught up with her, I squatted behind her and called her name again, and she stood, turned, and gave me a hug. Then she turned back to the headstone, squatted for a few seconds, stood back up, and turned and hugged me again. She repeated this scene one more time, and then ran off to play.

I couldn't get any explanation out of her—she had just turned two and her vocabulary was still very limited. But what other explanation can there be except that those were hugs from a brother whom I loved very much. He was only twenty-five when he took his life, but if he can send me a hug ten years after his death, I have to believe he is now at peace.

HANK

GLENDA F. KLIEWER

Every now and then someone will ask, "Have you ever seen a ghost?" I smile an affirmation and relate the following story.

It was five o'clock on an August day forty years ago. "Hi, Hank!" my little cousin's voice called merrily.

We were coloring on the front porch of our summer cottage near Lake Spavinaw in Oklahoma. The year was 1951, and for the five previous summers Henry Alan Nesbit Klark had served as art critic for the crayon pictures we created in our "quiet time" before supper.

That summer I was twelve and very sure of myself. I had always been infatuated with the handsome neighbor who lived in the large red-brick house at the other end of the resort known as Jade Hollow.

"Hi, Hank!" I said, looking up from my picture of sunflowers. He was as handsome as ever in his "Great Gatsby" three-piece suit with real gold buttons. His suit, because it was white, stood out in the green-ness of the afternoon. He smiled and reached into his pocket for his horn-rimmed glasses. I reached into my coloring box for another yellow, intending to ask Hank which would be the best color. When I looked up he was gone.

"Where did Hank go?" my cousin asked as she peeled some paper from her red crayon.

For an instant I had forgotten to remember that Hank was dead. My mom and dad had gone to his funeral. They had coached me that per-haps it would be better not to mention Hank's demise to my impression-able eight-year-old cousin.

"I'm not sure," I said. I knew that I couldn't tell my cousin who still believed in Santa Claus and the tooth fairy that she had seen a ghost.

My family sold the cottage the next year, and we moved to Kansas. In 1981 I made a special trip to Spavinaw to sit on the old porch. I sat for a long time squinting into the greenish air, looking toward the vacant red-brick house at the other end of the hollow. I stood up and yelled, "Hank! . . . Hank, where are you?"

As I walked to my car I turned for a final look at the scene of so many childhood memories. Sighing, I opened the door of my car and settled into the driver's seat. Adjusting my seat belt, I glanced into the rearview mirror.

For an instant I saw the reflection of the white suit, the gold but-tons, and the smile.

I turned to look. He was gone.

THE LAST TIME I SAW GRANDMA

SELDON A. PIERCE

The moonlight streamed through the curtainless windows, casting shadows across our bedroom. Lying there, awake, I felt the presence of something and smelled a sweet perfumelike odor. Turning on my back, I saw a figure moving about the room. It was darkly clothed and seemed to float rather than walk. The specter moved closer, bending over my bed. I could see her face clearly. An expression of concern came over her countenance, and a feeling of comfort mixed with fear came over me. The face was familiar; I had no reason to be afraid.

We lived in a three-room house in south Alabama and were dirt poor. My two brothers and I shared a bedroom, each of us sleeping on a separate cot. I was six years old when the visitation occurred.

My Grandmother Wilson died when I was eight months old. I can't remember seeing her. I felt I knew her, though, and thought of her a great deal. A picture of her standing beside my seated grandfather was hanging on the front-room wall.

As I lay in the bed watching, the figure went over to the bed of each of my brothers and bent over, observing them. Then the figure disappeared behind a long black coat hanging on a nail near my oldest brother's bed. She made no noise and seemed to touch nothing.

My mother was making biscuits when I went into the kitchen the next morning. "I saw Grandma last night," I told her.

Momma ignored me, opened the oven door, and placed the biscuits inside. "You had a dream," she said. "I do that sometimes."

Just then my middle brother came into the kitchen crying. This was unusual for a rough-and-tumble ten-year-old.

"What's wrong?" Momma asked. "Are you sick?"

"Something strange came into our room last night and hovered over me. I was too scared to move. I pulled the covers over my head and went back to sleep."

I had no idea anyone else had seen the strange apparition. My mother began to show interest in the subject.

My oldest brother burst into the room. He was excited. "Momma, you've got to move my cot. I saw Grandma last night. She went right through the wall where my bed sits." Virgil was thirteen. He remembered our grandparents well, as he had often stayed with them when he was a child. "Grandma was here last night. She checked each of us and left. I'm scared she might come back."

I was sure the phantom in our bedroom was Grandma. I was even more convinced when, a few years ago, I found a bottle of Hoyte's

Cologne in Bill's Dollar Store. The label on the bottle claimed that the cologne was made from a formula devised in 1886. I opened the bottle and smelled the fragrance. This was the odor I had smelled when Grandma came to visit her grandchildren in 1942.

None of us has seen her spirit again. We speculate about the visitation sometimes. We figure she could not rest until she knew we were all right. Satisfied, she left, never to return.

THE THREE-LEGGED TABLE

JAMES S. WILLIAMS

I never expected to tell anyone this story, let alone the whole United States, but it's true and maybe someone can figure it out.

I was born in Elmira, New York, which was a nice, normal place to grow up. Nothing strange happened to me before I was ten years old, and nothing strange has ever happened since that Saturday afternoon at my friend Kevin's house.

We had been to the picture show, and because it was late fall, night came early. Kevin and I were playing in his bedroom instead of outside, and his dad and mom were fixing up the kitchen.

Boys will be boys, so Kev and I had to supervise his dad as he lay on the floor under the kitchen sink. The drain was clogged, and he was cleaning it out. He had drained the water, taken off the elbow joint, and now had his head under the open drain, moving a wire hanger or something through the pipe to clear out the clog.

Kevin asked whether he could help, and his dad handed him the pot of water he had drained off and told him to get rid of it. Well, Kevin just emptied it back into the sink, and naturally it flushed down the drain and hit his father right in the face. Like a shot his dad was out from under the sink, and he started yelling at Kevin. It was then that things got strange.

Over in the far corner of the kitchen was an old-fashioned, three-legged table that Kevin's mom used for odds and ends. I believe that this little table was haunted.

It reacted to Kevin's dad's cussing. At first it just started shaking a little when he began to holler; then it began to move toward him—just kind of scraping slowly over the kitchen floor. I couldn't believe it was moving. I was speechless.

When Kevin's dad let out a big, loud curse, the table rose up about two inches and actually flew into him and then toppled over.

I stood there with my mouth wide open and my eyes bugging out of my head, but nobody else seemed concerned—Kevin's family had experienced this little three-legged table coming to life before.

They laughed and said that this was the first time a nonfamily member had witnessed its movement. Every time some member of the family really lost his or her temper and yelled or something, the three-legged table came to life until the person calmed down.

Kevin's mom said that the table was haunted by her great-grandmother, who had brought it over from Italy. She was supposed to have been very strict about cursing, and her ghost moved the little table to show her displeasure.

I never saw the three-legged table come to life again, and I often wonder whether Kevin's family still has it.

That's my ghost story. It's true and, as I said before, maybe somebody can figure it out.

JOCK'S HOME

MARILYN STOCKWELL

The stage was set for us to buy the house. I just knew we were meant to live there because of all the odd coincidences.

Although it was only eleven years old, the house had stood empty quite a while. A lovable old rascal named Jock had built the house and had really loved it. He had died there more than a year before. Many people had made offers to buy the house—it was a beautiful property on the lake—but all offers had been turned down. Finally, my husband and I came along and made a low offer, not daring to hope it would ever be considered. Then we heard that another party was driving up from downstate prepared to top our offer. But these people never appeared because they were involved in a car accident on the way. The house was ours.

Once again we looked through the place. It was entirely furnished—all was complete—there were even Kleenex and towels in the bathroom. The kitchen was fully equipped, right down to cocktail napkins. There were even clean sheets on the beds.

In the master bedroom, I pulled down the king-sized bedspread and discovered the same twenty-five-year-old threadbare Vera striped sheets that we owned. The telephone displayed the same phone number (except for the exchange) that we had had in our former home. Jock had been a watercolor painter; so was I. He had been a great golf and tennis enthu-. siast; so were we. Jock was a big Michigan State University football fan; so were we, as one of our sons had been a starter on the MSU team. Jock had also belonged to the same athletic club. In the cupboard we found glasses embossed with the club seal. Jock had been an inveterate duck hunter, as was my husband, whose business was running a duck-hunting lodge in Canada. Jock had owned a boat named *Odd Job*—we had owned a dog named Odd Job. Even the cocktail napkins in the drawer sported ducks and MSU motifs, the same as ours.

Jock had been likable, gregarious, and flamboyant. Everyone—even repairmen who came to the house—had stories to tell us about him.

The first night we stayed in the house, I was up late playing my piano, which had been delivered earlier. I had the strangest feeling that someone was standing by the doorway of the room listening to me play. It seemed like a person's shadow, but I knew it could not be my husband—I could hear the bed upstairs creaking as he turned over.

Soon after we unpacked our boxes and settled in, things started breaking and kept breaking. There wasn't an appliance in the house that didn't break down in some fashion and require attention. The dishwasher alone required five different service calls.

One night I was again up late washing a few dishes by hand (the dishwasher had quit again). Suddenly the hairs on the back of my neck rose as I felt a presence walk behind me and out to the hall. I turned and saw a shadow pass, heard a low chuckle, and smelled cigarette smoke. (My husband and I do not smoke.)

"Who's that?" I called.

No one answered. The shadow was gone. The distinct smell of a burning cigarette lingered in the air. I was beginning to suspect Jock was haunting our home.

We would go out to the store only to return and discover our cat, Stanley, who was an outdoor cat, inside the house. I checked all around wondering whether he had found a secret way in, but there was none. How did Stanley get inside?

I decided that Jock must be a friendly ghost who was just checking up on things and making sure we were taking good care of the house he loved so well. I posted a sign on the little blackboard next to the liquor cabinet: "Jock, please keep out of my Crown Royal." Often the sign would be erased by the next morning.

On another occasion, my new friend and neighbor, Toni, came by soon after we moved in. She seemed agitated, and later told me she had seen Jock that day up at the top of the stairs looking down at her. It had really upset her.

On three different occasions I was down on the lower level of the house painting when I heard someone come in the front door upstairs, walk through the hall, and go into the kitchen. Thinking it was my husband, Bob, returning with the mail, I put down my brushes and ran upstairs only to discover that no one was there.

One night we returned home late from a fishing trip. When we walked inside we discovered that Jock had paid us another visit. This time he had turned on his television set (which we had never used or even plugged in) and it was loudly emitting static. And, of course, there was Stanley, mysteriously enjoying the inside of the house, meowing a greeting at us.

Late on another night, as I was playing the piano again, I called over to the now-familiar shadow in the doorway, "Don't worry, Jock—I love your house, too, and I promise I'll take good care of it for you. I don't mind you being here sharing the house with us as long as you stay out of my Crown Royal!"

Not long after that, Jock seemed to fade away. Within a year after we had moved in, I felt he was gone. I missed his presence and speculated on why he had disappeared. Maybe he was finally satisfied that I would love his house for him. Or perhaps he was less than enchanted with my unskilled amateur piano concerts. Or, much more likely, could he have been disappointed that I wouldn't share my best whiskey with him?

A STRANGE WIND

GERALDINE GAWLE

It was about 4:00 a.m. My mother and I lay fast asleep in the same room and in the same bed with the door closed. All was quiet. Quiet, that is, until the sound of wind, a strange-sounding wind, awakened us. It seemed that we lay there forever, afraid to say anything, afraid of making a sound. I finally spoke and asked my mother what she thought those sounds coming from the kitchen were. She couldn't explain why the wind seemed to be only in the kitchen, and she had no idea what the sliding and bumping sounds were.

We lay there holding very tightly to each other, straining to hear, trying to keep our voices at a whisper and becoming more afraid. I asked whether she would get up to see what was out there, but I clung to her arm for fear that she might go.

She, in turn, asked whether I wanted to get up and see. Neither of us wanted to venture out from under the safety of the warm sheets. The sound of the wind continued, only from the kitchen, and the bumping sounds became louder. Days seemed to have passed, but actually the strange sounds lasted for about ten or fifteen minutes.

Without warning, the sounds stopped. We grabbed each other, gazed at the door, and held our breath. It now was so quiet that all that could be heard was the pumping of our hearts, sounding like muffled drums.

Then it happened! Ever so slowly, the large metal doorknob began to turn, and continued to turn for a very long time. It was as if the knob had grown and required extra time to complete a full circle. I know my mind went blank as my mother's probably did.

We must have sat up and leaned toward the turning knob without realizing it because as suddenly as it started to turn, it stopped turning, and we fell back onto the bed.

It was quiet again but only for a second. Suddenly the door flung wide open and banged against the wall, the knob smashing against the plaster. We both let out ungodly screams, jumped high off the bed, and stared at the door expecting to see a most grisly sight. The quiet surrounded us, and in the doorway stood absolutely nothing.

We shook ourselves as dogs do when emerging from the water and cautiously got out of bed. Everything in the kitchen was examined. Nothing was moved. All was in place except for one chair, which was standing away, carefully drawn from under the table as if awaiting someone. There were no signs of any other movement that would have explained the sounds. We sort of laughed and made our way back to bed. Sleep did not come easily for the rest of the night.

What was it? If I had been alone it could be chalked up to imagination. But this experience was shared with another adult. What was it that happened that night? What can turn a doorknob completely around and fling a door wide open?

Even stranger is that my mother and I were very close to my grandfather, my mother's father, who had recently died. We had to watch him die slowly, as there was nothing more the doctors could do. He died in the room directly next to where we slept that night. My mother and I were saddened by his death and, to comfort ourselves, had chosen to sleep that night in a bedroom that, when the door was open, looked directly onto the chair on which my grandfather had sat drinking coffee in the wee hours of the morning when he was unable to sleep.

The chair that was drawn from beneath the table was his.

A HUSBAND'S LOVE

JOANN SCHIANO

Not all ghost stories are frightening; some speak to the power of an enduring love. An old friend and fellow waitress told me the following story, which she swears really happened.

It started on perhaps the busiest day my friend ever had. The other waitress scheduled to work never showed up. There was no hostess or busboy, just my friend against a hungry world.

She figures she served twenty-two parties at one time—cocktails, appetizers, pasta, lobster, cordials, and on and on.

The temperature was ninety-one degrees outside, and it was unbearably humid. The temperature in the kitchen was probably ten degrees higher.

By the time she left work, her uniform seemed glued on. As soon as she reached home, she peeled off her clothes and jumped into the shower. No sooner was she out of the shower than the sweat started to pour off her again. So she put on a bathing suit and decided to spend the remainder of the evening swimming and floating in the ocean near her home and then drying off on the sand. She says she stayed at the beach for hours, until it grew very dark. A heavy thunderstorm was on its way, according to her little radio, so she left for home.

She fell into a very deep sleep as soon as her head hit the pillow. The activity of the day, no doubt, had finally taken its toll.

Later—she says she lost all track of time—she awoke to the crash of thunder. Lightning lit up all the windows of the house. Since it was impossible to fall back asleep right away, she went downstairs to get something warm to drink.

As she went down the stairs, she heard footsteps in the kitchen, and the clattering of dishes. A chill ran through her. After quietly tiptoeing to the kitchen, she peered in. There was her husband, placing a cup of tea down on the table and stirring it. He was a policeman, and that month he was working the night shift—she assumed that it was because she had been sleeping so soundly that she hadn't heard him enter the house. In her relief that he was not a burglar, she says she laughed loudly. At first he was startled by his wife's nervous response, but then he also began to laugh.

"Sneaking up on me, are you?" he asked.

He picked up my friend, ran into the living room with her in his arms, playfully tossed her onto the couch, and tickled her—she is uncontrollably ticklish and couldn't stop laughing. Then he kissed her.

"How's the restaurant? Busy these days?" he said.

"Today we were *very* busy. I was so exhausted I didn't even hear you come in. Then this terrible storm woke me up. I couldn't sleep. I felt chilly all of a sudden. I came down . . ."

"Come on, I've made plenty of tea for you, too."

"How was your shift? Any problems or arrests? Anything exciting to tell me?"

The couple walked back to the kitchen, and he poured her a cup of tea, the most delicious tea my friend had ever had. She normally didn't like tea, but she said that this tea tasted very good. It was strangely soothing to her mind and body.

"No, tonight was quiet, honey. A real piece of cake. I had a lot of time to think and talk to myself. I thought a lot about you and the children. I feel bad that you work so hard. It's rough having to support six kids these days. But we manage, thanks to your help. I really felt so restless for my shift to end, because I wanted to come home and tell you how much I appreciate and love you. You're an incredible woman, wife, and mother. I know you can do anything. I believe in you totally. I'll always love you more than anything else in the whole world. Thanks, darling!"

After this grand speech, her husband kissed and hugged her, and then he took her hand and kissed it. My friend says she was speechless and overwhelmed—she, of course, knew that her husband loved her deeply, but he was shy, not the type to verbalize his feelings.

"I love you too, honey," she responded. "I'm really happy that we work together so well. You and the children are my whole life. I'll always do my best for you guys."

Then her husband insisted that she go upstairs and get some rest. He carried her up the stairs, placed her back in bed like a baby, covered her with a blanket, and kissed her forehead.

"Sleep well, angel! I love you!"

"I love you, too."

She fell asleep instantly. It seemed that days had passed when she finally awoke. The sun was shining warmly on her face, and she felt very peaceful and rested—ready to serve forty-two parties at one time in the restaurant, if necessary.

As she went down to the kitchen to make coffee, my friend was surprised to see two cups in the sink and two tea bags in the garbage can. Suddenly the events of the past night came back to her, and she vividly recalled every word of the conversation with her husband. She started to chuckle as she remembered him carrying her up the stairs like a baby. Then just as quickly she began to cry uncontrollably—happy and sad all at once.

You see, my friend has been a widow for thirty-one years, ever since her young policeman husband was shot in the line of duty. She raised their six children by herself, supporting her family by waitressing.

In retelling this story, my friend seemed at peace. "I really enjoyed his visit," she told me, "because I miss him so much. I realize now that I wasn't ever alone—my husband was with me all the time. He gave me the strength and courage to believe in myself. That's why I could never remarry. I never lost him spiritually."

"Last night," she continued, "he came to tell me this himself, so that I'd know without question or doubt that together we had survived this physical separation and brought up our children with the greatest love and concern possible."

Nothing could ever separate the two of them. Never would my friend feel alone again.

THE GHOST WHO PLAYED THE VIOLIN

PATRICIA BRACKER

My mother still jokes about the stories we used to tell her when we were growing up in our one-hundred-year-old house in Michigan. To us, as children, the tales of footsteps with no one there, creaking floors, people standing beside our beds who disappeared when the lights were turned on, and something trying to pull our blankets off our beds were all very real. But we could never prove to our parents that any of them were true.

One experience, however, I shared with my mother, and she doesn't joke about that one.

On a cold December night in 1961, I shivered in my unheated upstairs bedroom, unable to sleep. In the distance, I kept hearing the faint, screechy sounds of strange music. I thought it sounded like the song "Ten Little Indians." Weird. The music seemed to be coming from inside my bedroom. I turned on the light beside my bed and looked around the room. No radio. No record player. I turned off the light. The music started again. This time the stairway door opened, and my mother yelled up to me.

"Turn that screechy music off. It's keeping me awake."

I waited until morning to question my mother about what she had heard. She repeated that the music had had a tinny sound, something like an old windup record player would make. She said she had even caught herself singing along to the tune of "One little, two little, three little Indians. . . ." She asked me why I was playing such silly music. I replied that I had heard the same music, but since I had no radio or record player, I could not have been playing the music. We decided that we wouldn't tell anyone about our experience.

Later I was curious about the history of the house and found a living relative of the man who had built it—his granddaughter. She told me that it had been built in the mid-1800s and was one of the first homes in the area. Originally, it had been a farm, which explained the numerous fruit trees in our yard.

But the big surprise came when I revealed my strange experience to the granddaughter. She listened quietly and motioned for me to follow her into the garage. She pulled out an old dusty box and produced a faded photograph of a bearded man holding a violin.

"This man was my grandfather," she said. "He built your house and loved it dearly. Before he died, he lived in your bedroom and used to tune his violin at night by playing 'Ten Little Indians.'"

A CHILD IN THE HOUSE

TRACY M. SABO

In the few years that we shared together, my brother Christian and I were very close. Every family photo ever taken of us showed us holding hands. He was always there for me. I know how much he loved me, and he knew I adored him.

At nine and a half, he was the oldest, and I was the only girl of four children, five years younger than he. We were the only kids in our family with hazel eyes, and our birthdays were only nine days apart. These things only added to our bond.

In 1961 on the Fourth of July, Christian, Danny (age seven), Greg (age three and a half) and I were all outside at our two-week-old new home in Florida. Christian was in charge of lighting all our sparklers—one after the other, keeping the laughter and enjoyment flowing.

Christian was killed in our new front yard the next day. He was struck by lightning. My sweet big brother, my best friend, was gone in an instant, forever—or so I thought.

One afternoon after we had moved to New Jersey, I came running into the kitchen and I saw my brother Evan, who was born three weeks after Christian's death, run out of the kitchen as I came in. I ran after him, calling, "Evan? What are you doing?" He ran through the hall and up the stairs, with me right behind him saying, "Stop it! Come here."

I went upstairs and searched every room but found the house empty. I was in a bit of a state of shock, especially when Evan came in from school an hour later and claimed he hadn't been home all day.

The little boy I chased had blond hair and was wearing beige shorts and a red, white, and blue striped shirt. Christian, who had short blond hair, was wearing beige shorts and a striped shirt when he was killed.

That summer many little incidents occurred, letting the family know that Christian was with us. For me, the best incidents were yet to come.

Off and on in various apartments of my own, away from the family, children's handprints appeared on my walls. Not once, not twice—many times. The prints looked as if they were made by someone who had first touched a newspaper—they were black and strong and visible to anyone. Sometimes you could see just a few fingers; other times the whole hand from thumb to pinky was there. Once the whole handprint appeared over my bed, right above my head.

Every single time these have occurred I've tried putting my hand into different positions to see whether I or someone else could have made them without realizing it. But every single time, the prints have been much smaller than my own hand. They seem to fit in my palm, maybe up to my rings.

Some time had passed since I'd seen a handprint, but then a few short weeks ago another appeared. I had just come out of a long relationship that left me sad and lost, because the breakup came about so suddenly. To cheer myself up, I was making myself get out with friends as often as I could. One night when I was out, I stepped outside to enjoy the stars and found myself silently speaking to God or the forces that be, asking for guidance at this time in my life. "Help me to know where I'm going now." And before I stepped back inside, I said to the sky, "Christian, if you can hear me, if you're still my big brother and guardian angel, please hold my hand. I need you now more than ever."

The next morning when I woke up there was a new handprint on the wall underneath the only childhood photo of myself I have hanging in my apartment. The print is very strong, very full—from thumb to palm to pinky—and fits inside the palm of my hand. I again put my fingers in various positions to see whether I could have made it. There haven't been any children around my house, and the print was not there before I asked Christian to take my hand again.

I must add that ever since the morning when the handprint appeared I've been relaxed and have been enjoying life and my newfound strength.

HAUNTINGS

GRANDPA'S SHOES

JO ANNE C. HEEN

My stepmother tells this tale:

"My grandparents on my father's side argued constantly. Grandma was a bossy lady who liked to have her own way, and no matter what Grandpa did, he couldn't please her. As they got older, he started to say, after every battle, 'When I die, I'm going to come back and haunt you.'

"The night he died, my grandmother phoned me to ask whether I would make all of the funeral arrangements. I agreed. One of the things I had to do was choose the clothes he would be buried in.

"My grandfather was a very neat man. Everything he owned had its place, and woe to the person who moved anything. Whenever we kids played at their house, we were always careful not to go near his closet and disturb his shoes, which were lined up neatly: the brown Sunday-best shoes, then his 'going-out shoes,' then his work shoes, and so on.

"When I picked out his funeral clothes, I debated which pair of shoes to take. I asked my grandmother, who told me to take the brown Sunday-best pair. Then she told me to throw the rest of his shoes away because no one in our family wore his size. I did as I was told.

"A few years later, when my grandmother died, I had the sad task of cleaning out her house. My mother warned me that I should go in the daytime, as Grandma always complained that Grandpa had come back to haunt her.

" 'She never slept well at night in that house after he died, you know,' Mother told me. 'She said that he walked around at night, keeping her awake, so she took to sleeping during the day.' As we both chuckled, my daughter, who was six at the time, said, 'I didn't like staying at Grandma's. People were always walking around in that house.' I explained to her that old houses creak as they settle, or when the wind blows, but I made sure it was bright daylight when I went over there.

"I spent the morning cleaning the downstairs, planning to tackle the bedrooms after lunch.

"When I opened the door to my grandfather's closet, there hung his suits, covered with dust. And there on the floor, in the same spot where they had sat for years, were Grandpa's brown Sunday-best shoes. The ones he was buried in. Covered with mud and green mold, the shoes were still wet, as if the owner had kicked them off only a moment ago. I didn't wait around to see whether his best suit was there, too."

SPECTRAL SAMPLER

L. J. PRUCHA

For me, growing up in northern Alabama was uneventful. About the scariest thing I knew was my grandparents' story about the Purple People-Eater, a monster that allegedly roamed the dark woods looking for lost children.

When it was time to start my first year of college, I decided to move to a place of my own. Luckily, or so I thought, I found a small, faded house within driving distance of classes. The rent was much lower than what I had expected to pay. The house met my basic needs—a place to sleep, eat, and change clothes as I rushed between classes and a couple of part-time jobs.

You'd think a haunted house would specialize in a particular phenomenon—rattling chains, flying spoons, slimy ectoplasm—but a mish-
mash of weird things started. I'm amazed I put up with the happenings
for two months. I had never experienced anything like it, nor have I seen
anything else like it to this day. It was as if whoever, or whatever, is in
charge of hauntings decided to randomly pluck an assortment of goodies
from a spectral sampler box. I didn't like any of them.

My mother and grandmother took advantage of the large backyard
and planted a vegetable garden. The corn, beans, tomatoes, cucumbers,
radishes, and even the okra developed black cancerouslike tumors. My
grandmother called it "smut," a disease she said was caused by too
much rain. The horrible harvest was left to rot.

It was true that there had been ample rain. One downpour oozed
through the ceiling of a bedroom, forming on the wall the unmistakable
shape of a gargoyle or a devil. The silhouette remained even after the
plaster dried. If I had stayed around longer, I might have tried painting
over the gruesome form.

The water piped to the house from a deep well periodically changed
to an unappetizing brownish red color. It tasted salty yet had no smell.
The elderly gentleman who was my landlord worked on the well pump
several times but could not find what caused the sudden changes in the
water.

Summer days in Alabama are hot, and summer nights seem to be
even hotter. The temperature in my bedroom was an exception. It was as
cool as if it were air-conditioned (or eerie-conditioned). There was a
corner of the room that was perpetually cold, with a chilling breeze
coming from absolutely nowhere. Although it sounds crazy, I continued
to sleep there. Several nights I awoke to find a shadowy figure at the
foot of the bed. It would stay only a few seconds and always disappeared
when I pulled my sheet up over my head.

One day as I rushed through the bedroom to change clothes and
head out to my afternoon job, I was showered with shards of glass. The
glass from an old painting had burst outward without disturbing the
picture or the frame. I stayed away this time for a couple of days before
I returned to clean up.

Not too long thereafter I met the former occupant. He and his family had rented for only two months. He said several of their pets had died, and there were too many strange things going on—but he said he didn't believe in ghosts. He had found out that there had been eleven renters before him in a five-year period. Let's see. That made him the twelfth, and that made me the thirteenth. . . . I clearly remember the chill that ran down my spine. It was time to move on.

When I returned to collect my possessions, I found my two kittens and my big white rabbit, Pearl, scattered in the front yard. They were dead, their throats ripped open. Neighbors said they had not heard anything, but there were rumors of a pack of wild dogs roaming the area. The bodies were still warm. There were no obvious signs of any parts being eaten. Just ragged gashes about their necks.

As soon as my belongings were hauled away, I did what my mother always did when we moved out of a house. I went back to sweep the floors. A strange ritual, actually. I never finished because a groaning sound began and got louder and louder as it seemed to move from room to room. It was so frightening that I got sick to my stomach. I dropped the broom and left the house.

I drove immediately down the road to return the keys to the landlord. Because I was still quite shaken, I decided to tell him what had happened. He was not surprised. He said he had given the house to his grandson about six years earlier as a graduation present. A few days later the young man had driven his motorcycle off a bridge and was killed instantly. The landlord told me that neighbors say they have sometimes seen a man standing in the front window when the house is not rented.

As I drove by the house for the last time, I couldn't help myself. I looked up the long driveway and there it was—a dark reflection of a man looking out of the front window. I pushed the accelerator as hard as I could and sped away.

THE SECRET DOOR

CLIFFORD B. BURNETTE

When I was a teenager, my family moved from a small town in southeast Texas to an even smaller one in northwest Tennessee. Dad, a very good mechanic, found work right away with a local farm implement company. The house we rented was small for us, as there were eight of us kids.

One day Dad came home with the good news that he had rented a much larger house outside of town. It was a well-kept, two-storied Victorian affair, surrounded by farmland and small groves of trees. Behind the house, and not more than thirty yards distant, was the mighty Mississippi River. Locals said that the house had been built in 1890 by a wealthy German immigrant. Because it was so close to the river, supplies could be conveniently conveyed to the house. After the farmer died, another individual took it over, and, because of its location and the large pier that had been built on the sandy shoreline of the riverbank, it became a hotel and casino. My father's coworker explained that many of the local people thought the place haunted. We scoffed at this idea. Besides, it had seemed like ages since we had had a home where we didn't feel cramped. It was just what we had been searching for.

The evening we moved in, Mom and Dad drove back into town to buy hamburgers for dinner. It was just about dark when they pulled out of the driveway. I suddenly turned to look at my little brother and six sisters and, pointing to one of my sisters, yelled, "Hide-and-seek! You're it."

Off we ran in various directions. I headed up the stairs and into a closet in one of the rooms. I closed the door and waited. I could hear below me each scream of laughter as one after another of the hiders was found.

A good while later, with the others in tow, my sister found me, but not before I had found something, too. I had noticed a hinged door that I would not have seen had I not been sitting so close to it on the floor of that closet. When my brother and sisters opened the door to the closet, there I was, busily trying to open the small door to see whatever lay beyond. The others watched as I finally managed to pull the tightly fitted door open.

It was at that very moment a blast of cold wind hit me square in the face. Inching forward, I peered into the darkness. Reaching in with my hand, I tried to feel for a floor, but found none.

Even though I was dying to know what lay beyond that small doorway built into the back wall of that closet, it would have to wait until I showed it to Dad. Besides, as I was thinking about my alternatives, one of my sisters was pointing out the window just a few feet away, telling us that Mommy and Daddy were back. We forgot about the secret door until after we had eaten our burgers and fries. By that time everyone was tired, and when I mentioned it, my father said it was probably an entrance to the attic. That night we were to experience our first unexplained and weird incident.

It was around ten that evening when everyone was finally in bed. In the next room and through the open door of the bedroom I shared with my brother, I could hear my parents as they lay in bed and talked. Then, suddenly, I heard what sounded like someone walking in the room directly above me. I thought for a moment that my father might have gotten out of bed to check on something upstairs. That thought was extinguished when I overheard my mother ask my father, "What in the devil was that?" Wondering about it myself, I crawled from bed and went into their room. By that time, Dad had turned the overhead light on and was getting dressed.

My father stepped into the hall, and, with me behind him, looked up the stairs. The moment he turned the main entrance light on, the footsteps from above ceased. Scratching his head, he walked back into his bedroom, me close behind, and pulled from beneath the bed the only gun we had in our house, a .22 caliber rifle. When he did this, I knew something must be up.

"What do you think it was?" I asked him. Looking at me he just said, "I don't know. Let's find out." With that, we walked up the stairs and through each of the rooms until we came to the room where the secret door was.

What sounded like a whistling wind was now coming from that closet. As we stepped closer, my father peered behind the closet door, hunching down on his knees to get a better look. I could see from where I stood that my father's hair was blowing gently in the breeze now emanating from the opening. Taking out his lighter and cupping it, he sparked a flame. Leaning forward, he tried to see into the space beyond. I could see that even with the wavering flame it was too dark to make anything out.

Just then, it felt as if a tremor pulsed through the whole structure of the house. It was slight, but just the same it caused my father to reach out and take hold of the door for support. "What was that?" I asked. He took his time in answering this question. "Probably the old place settling on its foundation," he said. I could tell by his reply that he doubted his own answer. After he had pushed the door to the passageway closed, he stood and looked at me, saying, "I don't want you kids to play in this closet. I'll board up the door to that opening tomorrow. Until then, keep the others out of this room."

Things remained quiet until later that summer, when we experienced a terrible storm. Strong storms accompanied by periodic tornadoes were not uncommon in that area, and, from the looks of it, we might be in for a real howler. Already we could see lightning on the horizon, snaking a path from the clouds to the ground. Little did we know that the house would bring us more fear than the storm ever could.

As my brother and I lay in bed, the lights out, we whispered about a trip we planned to take the next day, to Reelfoot Lake, where we could fish and swim. As we talked, so too did Mom and Dad, but about something entirely different. It seemed there was a light in their room coming from an unknown source. Apparently, it was not coming from a crack in the drapes, and they could find no source for the strange phenomenon. As Dad tried to find the source of the strange glow, the house suddenly shuddered rather loudly.

Both my brother and I sat up. At almost the same time, a heavy pounding began on the floor above us. This was too much for us, and we jumped from bed and ran into our parents' room.

"Go get your sisters up and bring them in here," Dad said to me, a look of alarm on his usually calm face. As I did this, the pounding above us seemed to grow louder and more violent. It was not hard to roust my sisters from their beds; some were already passing me on their way to the presumed safety of my parents' room.

With the last of us kids gathered at the foot of Mom and Dad's bed, the noise from upstairs suddenly stopped. We looked at each other in terror. "What is going on up there?" Mom asked Dad. My father didn't answer right away. He had already pulled on his pants and was now putting on his shoes. I ran back into my room to do the same.

I noticed that outside the window of my room, which opened onto the back porch, a light had begun to show through the curtains. As I watched, it grew brighter and brighter, intensifying to such a degree that it bathed the whole of the room in an eerie glow. Startled, I yelled out. Dad was in the room in a second. Walking over to the window to peer out, he moved the curtains aside. He looked out onto the porch for only a second before he dropped the curtain. "Come on," he said, looking toward the window. I didn't need to be told twice. We both backed out of that room and Dad closed the door behind him.

The pounding from above began again, this time with an increased frenzy. I looked from Mom to Dad—they were staring at each other as if in disbelief at what was now happening. The kids had piled around Mom in the bed, and some had even begun to cry. "I'm going upstairs to see what in the hell is going on," Dad said. "I'm coming with you," I responded. Hearing no objection to this, I followed Dad to the door. With the rifle in his right hand and his other hand on the knob, he opened the door and stepped into the hall. I was right behind him.

For a moment, we were in semidarkness; the only light was coming through the windows of the front entranceway at the other end of the foyer. I heard a click as Dad flipped the light switch on. Immediately I felt more secure. The pounding upstairs was still resounding throughout the house. As we looked up the staircase, contemplating what we knew must be done, the light in the hall suddenly went out. I heard my dad frantically trying the light switch. No good.

From the bedroom just on the other side of the door, we heard the startled cries of my sisters. They were not the only ones afraid, though I would be damned if I would show my own fear while in the presence of my father. "Go back into the bedroom. Now!" Dad exclaimed.

I was about to object, but I knew that tone of voice. My sisters, brother, and mother were all piled in the bed. I heard my mother trying to comfort the kids, but their hysteria was out of control.

Then, with the erratic noise from above taking on a new intensity, Dad came through the door. "Clifford, you get the girls ready to leave," he said to me. "Make sure they are all with you. When I open the door again, I want you to lead them and your mother through the hall and out the front doors. Get in the car and wait for me," he said quickly.

"What are you . . . ," my mother started to ask, but she was cut off by Dad.

"Be sure they all get in the car! Wait until I tell you," he exclaimed.

It took me only a few seconds to get the kids off the bed. I herded them to the door, waiting for Dad to give the go-ahead. "Now!" was all he said.

That was enough. Without looking back, I pushed the kids on ahead of me and into the hall. My mother was right beside me. The kids, then Mom, were out the door in seconds. I was just about ready to run out, too, when a strange and new sound reached my ears. It very much resembled the scream of a man in mortal pain. Turning, I looked to see whether Dad was behind me. It was then I saw something I have never been able to forget.

About halfway down the stairs was what looked to be a hazy, white form. It was actually pulsing—bright one second and dimming the next. In the middle of that hazy light stood what I believe was a man wearing what appeared to be a long coat. I could just make out his outline. I was stunned by the unexpected sight. My father was standing at the end of the stairs looking up at the thing, his gun raised, but not really aimed. Dad seemed to be trying to figure out what to do.

"Dad!" I screamed, wondering why he did not fire at whatever that thing was. It was as though he didn't hear me. I yelled again, this time louder.

The thing on the stairs was looking down at my father. It was saying something, but I couldn't make out the words. It was then that I saw another half-lit form appear around the bend at the top of the stairs. That was too much for me. With only a glance at the other thing, I turned and ran through the front doors and down the steps. The car was parked about ten yards away. I ran up to the driver's door, which was open, and jumped in. As I looked up and out the windshield of the car, I saw my father coming down the steps in a hurry.

I flung myself into the backseat, landing in the laps of the hysterical kids. Dad was now in the car and starting the engine. My mother was trying to find out what happened, but my father was too busy trying to get the old Rambler running. Finally, the engine turned over and caught. Not waiting for the car to warm, Dad put it in gear. I looked back at the house as we drove quickly away. My dad must have left the front doors open, because I could see several white shapes in the hallway as the car raced down the driveway to the gravel road. I didn't know it until later, but Mom had also seen the figures.

We drove through the rain and into town that night, pulling into its only truck stop. My father parked the car and went in, leaving us alone and still shaken. A short time later he returned with a cardboard tray of coffee and hot cocoa. Handing us each a cup of hot liquid, he told us to sit back and relax.

We stayed parked in the lot of the truck stop until sunrise. Driving back to the house made all of us apprehensive. We didn't know what to expect when we got there. As we drove into the yard, everything looked normal enough. My father and I got out and went inside. I noticed that the doors were closed, but the wind could have done that, I thought. As we entered the hall, there was only the sound of our own footsteps against the polished hardwood floors. We went directly to the stairs and started up. I remembered the rifle back in the car.

We went through each of the upper rooms, finding nothing out of the ordinary until we came to the room that had the closet with the door inside. The door to the closet itself looked as if it had been torn from its hinges. Parts of it were strewn about the floor of the room. Neither of us spoke as we surveyed the damage. Stepping closer to the closet, we looked inside and saw that the hinged panel that opened into that other mysterious area of the house had also been torn loose and was now hanging by only one bent hinge. "What could have done that?" I asked, awed by the sight.

"I have no idea; it could have been the storm last night, I suppose," Dad replied. I knew that he knew better than that. We stood there a little while longer and finally went back downstairs and searched the rest of the rooms in the house. We found nothing out of place below.

That day we drove into town and found another place to rent. When the new landlord asked why we were moving from the large house on the river, my father told him that it was because it was too far from the school and his job. The landlord offered to help us move; he had a large, open grain truck. My father gladly accepted the offer. By sundown we had hastily packed everything we owned into the truck and left that house. My father told me sometime later what the landlord had said about the place.

"I'd seen you folks moving in when I passed by. I wondered how long it would be afore you left. Seeing all them children, I knew it wouldn't be long. I was right again," he had said to my father.

When Dad had asked him what he meant by "right again," the man told him we weren't the first ones to move in and out of that place.

"Folks around here believe that place to be haunted," he told my father.

"What do you think?" my father had asked him.

"I should be asking you what you think. You're the one who moved," the landlord replied to my father's questions.

Many years have passed since then, and now there are eleven of us kids. We are all grown and have families of our own. Those of us who remember our mansion by the river sometimes bring it up when we're together. My father rarely gets involved with our discussions about that house, preferring instead to sit and listen. I have asked him on a couple of occasions what he thought it might have been that we experienced that evening. He just smiles and says, "Oh, I don't know. Could have been the wind. Could have been any number of things."

I thought of going back to the old place but found out that the house, along with a few other ones in the area, had burned to the ground.

A WANDERING GHOST

SHERRILLE J. HAYSE

We had just moved into a very pretty modern home that was only about two years old at the time.

The mysterious occurrences started about a month afterward. I'd be watching television or sitting at the dining room table and I'd hear someone speaking my name. At first I ignored the voice because it happened only once in a while, and only when I was alone. When the children or my husband were home, I didn't hear it.

My husband, a truck driver, was gone a lot, so I thought my ears were playing tricks on me when he was away and just put it down as nerves.

As each month went by, we fell more in love with the house. I was often upstairs to keep the kids' bathroom clean and to make sure that they were keeping their rooms clean. Half the time, I ended up cleaning their rooms myself. Eventually the ghost started following me upstairs, calling and whispering my name. One time it was so close to me that I became frightened and went back downstairs in the middle of my daily chores, just to calm down. It was at that point I felt that maybe, just maybe, I was going crazy. The voice never seemed to bother anyone else but me.

I was curious about the kids' bedroom doors. It seemed that every time I shut their doors during the day, their doors would be open when the children came home from school. Sometimes my daughter would start an argument, accusing her brother of being in her room and moving things around. Sometimes things would disappear one day and show up a few days later.

In the meantime, doors would open and close at night. We'd be asleep downstairs and all of a sudden my husband and I would both wake up and feel that someone was in the room. For several months I got very little sleep. On the nights my husband was gone, I would get to the point that I'd be too frightened to close my eyes. But the children loved the house, and they never complained about anything strange going on.

One day the kids and I went to the store, leaving my husband at home. While we were gone, the ghost started in on him. He heard the sound of footsteps up and down the stairs and saw the front doorknob shaking like someone wanted in—or the ghost wanted out.

When we arrived home from the store, my husband was as white as a sheet. He said he had heard the ghost three or four times. We all decided to look for another place to live. We realized that there was a presence in our home, and it wasn't going to go away.

Every day after that when I sat down at the dining room table, I could hear the ghost breathing and letting me know that it was there. I tried to ignore it until finally, one night, it went after my husband. That same night I woke up in the early hours of the morning in a cold sweat. I could sense that the ghost was in our bedroom.

The next morning when my husband was in the bathroom shaving, I went up and gave him a bear hug from behind. I was shocked to see four scratches on each of his shoulders. Big, long scratches! I didn't have long nails and he kept his nails very short, so we both knew the scratches didn't come from either of us. I always gave my husband's back a once-over, and I knew he didn't have those scratches the night before. We started worrying about our children; I was afraid that the ghost would go after them next. We continued looking for another place, and by the time we found one, I was a nervous wreck.

Nothing happened after that except on the day I packed up. The ghost started whispering my name again. I cried and told the ghost that he or she could have the house back. I told it I loved the house, but I loved my family more and that we wouldn't be back.

About a month after we moved out, my children told me that the presence had bothered them, too, and that sometimes it would shake their beds so hard that they woke up at night. My nephew verified that the bedroom doors were being opened by something. He said that the night he spent with us he was alone upstairs taking a shower, and the bathroom door kept opening while he was in the shower. He said it scared him, but he thought it was his imagination. All of the kids had been too frightened to talk about it until we left the house.

Later on, I talked to several people who lived in the area long before the house was built, and they said that several people had drowned in the big lake near where the "haunted" house stands.

The house we now live in is about one hundred years old, and so far there is no evidence of the wandering ghost. What a relief.

THE CAT WHO LIKED TIES

MICHAEL FADDEN

My wife is one of those people who have a place in their hearts for stray animals. I, on the other hand, am one of those people who don't like cats. So I was less than pleased one evening when my wife came home with a stray cat, which she named Boomer.

Well, ol' Boomer and I didn't hit it off. I have a habit of hanging my neckties over the door handle of my closet door, and it just so happened that Boomer quickly turned my ties into hanging pieces of exercise equipment. He would work off his feline love handles by jumping up and clawing my ties. Too stubborn or too stupid to simply fold my ties and put them into my dresser drawer, I used my shredded ties as a tangible argument why Boomer had to go.

After about six weeks and four or five ties destroyed, our landlord received a mysterious anonymous note saying that the young couple in apartment 7-B were keeping a pet cat. Since having a cat violated the terms of our lease, we shipped Boomer off to live at my in-laws' farm. What a shame.

Unfortunately, Boomer was hit by a pickup truck two weeks later. My wife took it pretty hard. My period of grieving was a bit shorter.

Weeks passed and I was enjoying a pleasant night's sleep, not battling my wife for control of the blankets as she was out of town for a few days on business. I had a brand-new tie hanging on my closet door, and all was right with the world. Then I was awakened by that familiar scratching sound on the closet door, just as I had been many times before.

Seconds later, reality struck, and I sat straight up in my bed. Boomer was now residing in kitty heaven—so what was making the noise? Just then, and I swear it to this day, I saw that familiar white tail dash out of the bedroom.

My heart began to pound. I turned on the lights and ran to the closet. I grabbed my four iron out of my golf bag and searched the entire apartment, feeling like I was in the middle of a Stephen King novel. As I bent down to look under the sofa, golf club firmly in my grip, I expected a crazed wildcat to dart out and sink its silk-covered claws into my throat.

Ten minutes later, after finding absolutely nothing, I sat on the edge of the bed and laughed at myself. A grown man allowing his imagination to run wild, like a teenager staying alone for the first time.

I returned to my slumber.

The next morning, I laughed again at myself as I got dressed for work. But as I stood in front of the mirror putting on my tie I looked down and . . . and it was shredded at the bottom! This was a new tie! I don't think I took my next breath for at least seven minutes.

I picked up my wife at the airport that night. I was too embarrassed to tell her my story.

Weeks have passed since that one bizarre night. But my wife's going to be away again in a couple of weeks. I think I'll put my ties in my dresser drawer, and maybe I'll share the blankets with my four iron. Just in case.

A PRESENCE OF EVIL

NANCY L. WHITAKER

In 1973 we bought a small house in a nice section of a small town in western Kentucky. The house wasn't that old—it was built in 1934—and we were only the second owners (we bought it from the second wife of the man who built the house).

The things that occurred there happened only occasionally, and different things happened to different members of the family. We were not aware of all of each other's experiences until after we moved, some thirteen years later.

My own experience left me shaken for a long time. At approximately two o'clock one morning, I was awakened from a sound sleep. No apparent reason. I had not been dreaming. The bed faced a doorway into the hall, and the door was open. In the doorway I saw a figure dressed in a long robe, possibly with a hood. All I could see, other than the black outline, was a shining glow where a face would be.

I was petrified and found myself unable to move. I seemed to be paralyzed. I kept telling myself I had to be dreaming and, if I could just awaken my husband lying next to me, everything would be all right. All I can say is that there was a feeling of extreme evil that seemed to be coming from the figure. After several attempts to speak my husband's name—my voice seemed to be paralyzed, too—I finally croaked out "John." I managed to say my husband's name a second time, and finally a third time. Each time I said "John" the figure became smaller, and it disappeared completely when my husband woke up.

I was shaking from head to toe, my paralysis disappearing with the vision. My teeth were chattering so badly that I was unable to speak coherently for many minutes. My husband is a realist and kept trying to find a logical reason for the apparition—the streetlight, headlights, neighbors' lights—but he never could convince me that what I had seen was a normal phenomenon.

I used to get peeved at my son Ed because when I went to his room to awaken him for school or work he was never there. Usually I would find him on the couch in the den. About a year after we moved he told me the reason he would never sleep in his own room: he was terrified in there. He had been awakened on many occasions, usually in the early morning hours, with the feeling that someone was in the room, even though he could see no one. During these times he would be paralyzed, unable to move a finger, for many terrifying minutes. On several occasions he was awakened by being lifted bodily from the bed and dropped. He never saw anything. He just had the feeling of a presence in his room, and the only good night's sleep he ever had was on the couch in the den.

After hearing this, I began to quiz my other children to see whether anything had ever happened to them in this house. My son Mike, before going into the navy, had had the same bedroom that Ed had his experiences in. He told me that on one occasion he was awakened from a sound sleep early in the morning to see a figure at the end of his bed, just looking at him. He describes it as an old lady in a gown and bathrobe. After several seconds he turned on the lamp by the side of the bed, at which time the apparition disappeared. His words triggered a memory I had of a conversation with the lady next door. I had asked her one time why the second Mrs. McOwen had sold this house and bought one only a few blocks away, a house very similar to this one. She had confided in me that Mrs. McOwen was scared in this house.

Ed and Mike were using the same bedroom that the first Mrs. McOwen had died in. She had been upstairs in what was now our bedroom until a terminal illness left her unable to manage the stairs.

Several years after our move, my husband, the realist, made the remark that he had not had one of those terrifying nightmares since leaving our old house. I looked at him in surprise because I, too, as well as Ed, had had horrible, vivid nightmares in that house. They always seemed to involve murder, rape, cruelties of all sorts—they were the kind of dreams that leave your heart pounding and your body shivering. Since we moved out, we all have observed that we no longer have these nightmares, only normal, everyday dreams, like everyone else.

A THOUSAND OR MORE HAUNTED NIGHTS

JOYCE PRESTRIEDGE

Where do I begin? Which eerie experiences should I relate? Should I mention that there were very few nights (or days) that *something* didn't occur?

Should I say that my childhood home was inhabited by a family of seven, various pets, and three (possibly four) entities? I will mention that as a born-again Christian it was very difficult to reconcile my religious belief with ongoing supernatural occurrences.

When I was in the sixth grade my family moved into an almost new house in a countrylike suburb of a large city. The original owners had suddenly moved, having lived there only a few months. It was love at first sight for my family. The home had all the features we wanted, and some we hadn't even dreamed about.

Strange things started happening almost as soon as the ink was dry on the closing documents. We adjusted to the almost daily occurrences and, over time, even developed a relationship of sorts with the other inhabitants of our home. We could tell which entity wanted attention by the type of prank performed. They were never shy. It didn't matter whether other relatives or friends were present—if the spirits wanted to remind you of their existence, they did!

On one such occasion, my girlfriend Barbara was spending the night. Like most teenage girls, we giggled a lot before and after lights-out. My parents had to shush us more than once, but finally we settled down. As I was drifting off to sleep, Barbara asked why I was pulling the covers down. I responded by saying it was probably George, because that was the trick he always played on my grandmother when she visited. It was one of his favorite pranks. Barbara didn't believe me until she realized I was speaking from my bed across the room. There was no way I could have reached her bed, much less pull the covers off.

Barbara immediately bounded out of bed, insisting it was a trick while turning on the lights. To help calm her, we decided to push the beds together in the middle of the room. Lights off, we settled back down and tried to sleep. Again the covers of Barbara's bed were pulled down.

This time it was very hard to calm her. I turned on the lights and explained in greater detail about our resident ghosts and their idiosyncrasies, all the while assuring her that it had to be George because he liked to tease. He never truly harmed or terrified you. While talking, we returned the furniture to its original position. We left one light on, and this time she got into bed with me. We believed the rest of the night would be uneventful.

Suddenly, the bed began to bounce. Our bodies were held rigid, and we bounced higher and higher, a good six inches off the bed. It felt as if we were on a trampoline. We were scared stiff.

Finally my father entered the room demanding we quiet down because we were disturbing the whole household. As he entered the room the bed stopped bouncing. Hysterical, we raced from the room.

Barbara called her parents and went home immediately. Even though we have been friends for more than twenty-five years, Barbara never visited that house again, not even during the day.

Years later, one sunny Saturday afternoon in the spring, my mother phoned and asked my husband and me to come over as soon as possible. Because we literally lived around the corner, we arrived at my parents' house in less than three minutes, fearing bad news. As we entered, mother led us down the central hallway to their bedroom, relating a most unusual story. This particular day all my younger sisters were gone for the entire day and evening. Mother felt it would be the perfect time to wax and buff the hardwood floors. After they were done with the floors, my parents had indulged in an afternoon nap. Upon awakening, they noticed what appeared to be white, powdery footprints around their bed. They followed the prints from their room through the hall and into my old bedroom. The footprints originated and stopped under the ceiling light, in the middle of the room.

It looked as if something had dropped from the ceiling, walked to my parents' room, and examined them as they slept. Then it had returned to my room, exiting, as it had entered, from the middle of the floor.

As we examined the narrow three-toed prints (about the size of my hand), they began to fade. Looking at them more closely, I leaned against the utility closet in the hall. Suddenly we heard a spine-tingling noise—like long nails pulled across a blackboard—coming from the closet. Simultaneously I felt a searing pain ripping through my arm, and I reeled away from the closet door. I staggered as if from a blow, and my husband halted my fall to the floor. My mother noticed a deep, bloody scratch extending from just below my shoulder to just above my elbow.

I had to physically stop my husband from opening that closet door.

He had never believed any of the family stories, and consequently had had trouble comprehending our true situation. I knew if he opened the door a force would be unleashed that we couldn't control. Deep terror welled within me as I realized that this was the one entity that was truly evil. He would injure you if given the chance. Before, he had always been held in check by a white light that would appear on the ceiling, moving until it was directly over my head.

The white light was like a guardian. Warmth, peace, strength, and security would envelop you like a welcomed cocoon when it was present. You knew you were safe from anything and everything.

But the white light hadn't appeared. We were on our own. Because of previous contacts, I knew that this horrifying presence did not have access to the whole house. Our safety was distance. Our escape from the hall was immediate.

Within twenty minutes of our arrival, the journey into terror had ended. Relative normalcy had returned. The footprints had completely vanished. Mother's floors were shining, unmarred. The mark on my arm had also disappeared without a trace.

That chapter, like so many others, closed with a concrete faith in God and a prayer that He would keep us safe from things that go bump in the night.

MOTHER AND HER TV

CAROLYN YOUNG

I was not a strong believer in the supernatural until something happened that shattered my complacency. I now believe that some people with very strong personalities have the power to come back from the dead and communicate with us. The incident that I shall relate occurred right after my mother passed away.

Before starting the story, however, I should mention that my mother strongly disliked my husband; he had told her to "shut up" one too many times. No one told Mother to shut up.

After Mother fell and broke her ankle, she went into a convalescent home to recuperate. While waiting for her to get well enough to go home, I paid the rent on her apartment. But Mother eventually decided that she was not going to get well and refused all medication and physical therapy. She died in January 1977 at eighty-two years of age.

After she was gone, we put most of her furniture into storage, except for her television set, which had been in good working order when she had her accident. We put it in our bedroom and hooked it up to our cable system. When we turned it on it would work for a while and then suddenly go black.

I called our reliable television repairman, who arrived during our dinnertime and headed for the bedroom. When we finished dinner, he was still working on the set. "There's nothing wrong with this set," he told me, but he'd get it working and poof, out it would go again. He finally got it to stay on, and it was working when he left. I turned it off, glad that the repair turned out to be nothing serious.

I turned the television set on the next day, and to my amazement smoke started pouring out of the back of it. I pulled the plug immediately, thinking it was going to explode at any moment. We decided it was not worth spending any more money on it, and so we planned to store it with the rest of Mother's furniture.

Before we got it out of the house, I moved it while dusting. I heard a loud crack and looked down to see that one of its legs had broken—the right one, about two inches from the bottom. Because there was no apparent reason for that leg to break, I was now completely shaken, my imagination running rampant. My mother also had broken her right leg.

At that time I was going to a therapist, who was helping me get through my mother's illness and death, as well as other ongoing problems. She was a very down-to-earth, levelheaded person. Since I was really shaken by these events, I told her about them, expecting to be told that everything was explainable and that this was all a natural reaction to my mother's death. The first words out of her mouth were, "Get rid of that television set." Needless to say, we did.

PYROTECHNICS

JACKIE HEARTH

We heard strange tales about our new home: Mr. Aloysius, the former owner, had tried to kill his wife many times but never succeeded. Then he tried to do himself in. He took to jumping out into the highway in front of speeding cars. But it was the gas stove in the kitchen that finally took him to ghostland.

Friends asked us whether we minded moving into his house, but we were thrilled to find a six-room house with a garage and a screened-in porch within our limited means. Baby number three was on the way, and we needed space. Besides, we'd never met Mr. Aloysius and felt he'd have no animosity toward us.

We found balled-up newspapers and boxes of wooden matches scattered under the loose floorboards in the attic. We laughed and took them to be evidence of another one of Mr. Aloysius's suicide attempts that failed. He had done the same thing in the basement, nailing up sheets of plywood to hold the newspaper in place. Gradually, my husband was clearing out the mess.

One afternoon when the children were napping, I was in the basement doing the laundry and heard footsteps coming from my daughter's room—the room that had been Mr. Aloysius's. I ran up the stairs to chase my daughter back to bed, but she was sleeping soundly. It became a regular routine when the house was quiet: I heard the footsteps, always coming from that room and going to the back of the house.

I tried telling my amusing ghost story to friends but was usually patted on the head, and mumbling went on about the vagaries of pregnant ladies and the settling of old houses.

My husband was very kind, but he acted superior—until he had to stay home to care for the children while I was in the hospital delivering the new baby. He looked very contrite when he confessed to having heard the same footsteps several times. Since he thinks curling up with a balance sheet is exciting, everyone started to give some credence to our story. We still were not frightened.

Easter weekend, when the baby was four months old, we went to stay with my parents. While we were there I dreamed that our house burned down. I said nothing but was very relieved to see all was well when we arrived home.

My mother had given the children some chicks. It turned cold that night so we put them in a large box and set it near the furnace. I said, "We won't have a fire, will we?" Five hours later I heard the baby fussing in the next room. I turned on the light and saw that there was smoke less than a foot above our heads. I called the fire department while my husband gathered up the children—we barely escaped.

Later the fire chief assured us that the placement of the box of chicks had had no bearing on the start of the fire. In fact, the firemen simply could not pinpoint why and how it started. But they were sure that we would not have escaped if we'd left ten minutes later, because the walls themselves were a huge firetrap. We hadn't realized that they were full of paper and matches, too.

We rebuilt the house and moved back in, confident that the ghost had used up his venom. We lived there five more years without incident. Unless you want to count the time that I suddenly felt myself pushed down the stairs. I hadn't fainted and didn't trip. It didn't seem worth worrying about. Oh, yes, and then there was the time . . .

ONE OCTOBER NIGHT

MARY FELDMAN

It was late on a stormy October night. The wind howled. Rain pelted against the windows. Piercing swords of lightning stabbed menacingly at the ground, creating brief bursts of day out of night. Rolling thunder caused the house and its sole occupant, me, to tremble.

A levelheaded person, I knew there was nothing to fear, that the storm would soon abate and peace would return; yet there is something unsettling about an autumn storm in the dark of night.

I was restless, uneasy. I sensed something, an undercurrent of sinisterness that alerts and alarms even the sensible.

Like candles in a draft, the lights flickered and dimmed, which made reading difficult; so I put my book aside. Yawning and stretching, I went upstairs to retire for the night.

Entering the bedroom, I noticed that the bedside clock on the nightstand was not working because of the storm. The bright red digits blinked like a stoplight in the wee hours. Over and over the same numbers flashed—11:48 . . . 11:48. Anxious for sleep, I decided to wait until morning to reset it. I looked at my wristwatch. It was 12:10 a.m.

As I went down the hall to the bathroom the lights were steady, the storm quieting as I turned on the faucet and began my nocturnal ritual. Remove makeup, wash face, brush teeth.

The house was peaceful. Only a distant roll of thunder or an occasional creaking in the eaves broke the silence. I was no longer apprehensive but relaxed and ready for sleep.

I was blotting the last vestige of makeup from my face with a tissue when I heard it. I stopped my ministrations to listen. Plop . . . plop . . . plop . . . the noise was coming from an area directly behind me.

Even sensible people are anxious about the unexpected. I turned around but not too fast. I wasn't in a hurry to see what was making the sound. I stared for a long moment, examining the built-in linen closet that held towels and spare bedding. Hands trembling, I cautiously opened one of the two doors.

I examined the shelf in front of me. Nothing there. I was both relieved and ashamed of myself for being such a scaredy-cat.

Plop . . . plop . . . plop. I moved my eyes upward toward the top shelf where extra pillows were stored. An exclamation of shock escaped my lips as I watched drops of coppery red fluid coming from a crack in the trapdoor that led to the attic.

Mesmerized, I stared as a rouge stain spread over the absorbent cloth of a pillow. Blood! Blood? Of course not! It couldn't be. Or could it?

Common sense took control. Reason overcame terror. The dripping red stuff surely was not blood. The wind-driven rain must have caused water to seep under the shingles into the attic. As for the bloody color, well, the water probably ran over a rusty pipe or something.

Still, I'm only human. The lateness of the hour, the wind, the storm, all the ingredients were there to activate my imagination.

Silly, childish woman! Too many horror films. Too much *Poltergeist*. Too much Stephen King. It's only rusty water. A perfectly natural phenomenon in an old house after a storm.

I took a deep breath to relieve the tension. Calmer now, I removed the pillows and placed an old towel under the drip to absorb the moisture.

The plop . . . plop was irregular now and soon would stop altogether.

"No boogeyman is going to get me," I told myself as I flipped off the bathroom light and went down the hall to the bedroom.

I crawled under the covers and reached over and turned off the light. Eyes wide open, I lay there in the dark looking at the bright red digital numbers on the electric clock: 12:33.

12:33? No winking? No blinking? No 11:48? Did the clock correct itself? Had I only imagined it had stopped? Or perhaps in my nervousness I'd reset it and forgotten.

"I can't think about it now," I thought. "I'll figure it out in the morning."

I continued to lie there listening—for what, I don't know. The plop . . . plop had stopped. A blowing tree branch brushed against the window. I reached over and turned the bedside lamp back on. Finally, I dropped off to sleep.

At 7:15 a.m. a weak autumn sun lit the east window. I threw back the covers and, humming softly, made my way to the bathroom. The terror born of the darkness was gone.

The pillows were on the floor where I'd left them a few hours ago. Seeing them brought to mind the happenings of the night before.

I looked up at the ceiling and froze. The red globs were no longer dripping, but the trapdoor to the attic was open, exposing a gaping rectangular blackness.

What really happened on that stormy October night? The plop . . . plop of rust-colored liquid dripping from the attic, the electric digital clock that set itself, and the open trapdoor—surely, there's a rational explanation, but I have never found one.

HE WANTS WHAT IS HIS

SHERRI KENOBBIE

In October 1973 we had been married for about a year. I was seven months pregnant, and because my husband, John, had problems finding a job, we were staying with John's sister. John's grandmother proposed another solution. She suggested that we live in her house temporarily and do the remodeling it needed. She would stay with her daughter until the work was done. We agreed.

The old, two-bedroom white house faced a cemetery. The interior had been stripped of everything except the sinks, stove, and bathtub. We moved our bed, television set, table, and two chairs in, but the house still echoed with so much emptiness.

The basement, which had a dirt floor, seemed just big enough for the old coal furnace that was being dismantled piece by piece and taken up the old wooden stairs to be junked. It took ten days to install the new furnace, and when it was in place we decided to go downstairs and check it out. We had been standing there a few moments when John spotted two old trunks, almost completely covered with coal dust and spiderwebs. Carefully John pulled them closer to the dangling light bulb.

John opened the first trunk—it had old tablecloths, doilies, and scarves in it. The second trunk John had problems opening because the hinges had rusted. When he finally got it open, he kneeled down beside it and became very quiet. The trunk was full of his dad's belongings—a pilot's uniform, hat, and several other personal things.

His dad's plane had crashed about ten years ago in the canyons. Nobody ever found his body, just the plane.

John removed the hat and shut the trunk. He went upstairs and hung it up over our bed.

Later that night, John's friend Tim came to visit and told us that his company had permanent work for John. Things were starting to look much better for us.

But everything wasn't all right. In fact, it all started that night. At 3:00 a.m. I awoke from a dead sleep to unintelligible chanting. I tried waking John up, but before I succeeded the chanting stopped.

The next morning I asked John whether he had heard anything unusual, and he said no. He went off to his new job, leaving me his work number to call if anything should happen.

Every night for the next two weeks the same chanting went on. It always began at 3:00 a.m. and lasted thirty minutes. John never heard it. I was really getting tired of this noise, and it was making me very nervous. John was annoyed with me for waking him up every night.

When John finally told Tim about the noises I was hearing, Tim offered to put us in contact with a psychic he knew. Three days later, Marianne arrived. As soon as she walked into the kitchen, she told us, "There's no need for me to go any farther. There's a spirit here, but it's too large for me to deal with. It's greatly disturbed and upset."

John's mouth dropped open. I was relieved to have somebody believe me. Marianne was ready to leave after being there only a few minutes.

That night I slept all night—no more noises! Maybe Marianne had done something to get rid of it!

The next morning I got John off to work and was going to walk to the Laundromat, but it had snowed all night. So I decided to go back to bed.

Everything was so quiet that I fell right asleep. All of a sudden the wind came up, and the clacking of the branches against the house woke me. I lay there for a few minutes and then relaxed. But there it was again, the chanting. It got louder and louder, and I was so scared that I couldn't move. I felt as if I were frozen. I thought that because nobody was there to protect me it would get me and I would die. But as quickly as the chanting started, it stopped.

Then the basement stairs began to creak, one by one. Somebody was in the basement, I thought. The basement door opened, and then the footsteps stopped. It sounded as if a cat had jumped onto the Formica-topped kitchen table. I heard what sounded like the scratching of claws, as if somebody had knocked the cat off the table. The footsteps got closer and now came from the living room. A few more steps and whatever it was would be in the bedroom.

I can't leave now—it's too close for me to get out of here, I thought. Do I lie here and pretend I'm asleep? Will it know I'm really awake? Is it going to get me? Is it going to leave? Oh God, I prayed. Please God, help me, save me! The bedroom door opened; I froze. I didn't even breathe.

It stood in the doorway—it just stood there. What does it want? Why is it doing this to me? I asked myself. The bedroom door slammed shut. Then the kitchen door.

I jumped out of bed and ran out of the house to the neighbors. I couldn't quit shaking. The neighbor called the police first and then called John.

The police arrived and thoroughly checked the house inside and out. Nobody was there. They told me that there were no tracks in the snow either. Nothing was downstairs—just a lot of spiders. "There's nobody here," they said.

John arrived as the police were leaving. I was still in tears. To reassure me, he looked around, too.

I got dressed, and John took me over to my girlfriend Carolyn's house. Carolyn and I sat there talking and drinking hot chocolate for at least two hours. We decided we had better do our laundry anyway. We got into her car and stopped off at my house to pick up my laundry.

I made her go into the house with me because there was no way I was going into that house by myself! We walked in, side by side, stopping in the doorway to see whether there was anything there. My laundry was in the back bedroom, off the kitchen. As I was stuffing my laundry into the bags as fast as I could, Carolyn went and stood by the basement door. "So it opens doors, too?" she asked. "Yes, come on let's go," I shouted. "Wait," she whispered. "Listen, there's somebody on the stairs." Carolyn was only two feet from the door when it opened. We screamed. There stood a huge black thing, just a mass of blackness, no body—just black stuff!

We were still screaming as I grabbed for Carolyn and we ran to her house. I called my husband again; he was really mad now. But this time we had both seen it.

John got to Carolyn's and told Tim to get ahold of the psychic again. It was almost dark outside when Marianne, the psychic, arrived.

We walked into our house. This time Marianne went into our bedroom. "He wants what is his," she said.

John and I both stood there for a moment, looking at each other. Then John walked over to where he had hung his dad's hat, took it down, and put it back into the trunk in the basement. Then he pushed the trunks back into the corner, just to be on the safe side.

It was two weeks before we finished the work on the house, and nothing else ever happened.

THE SHADOW OF DEATH

THE OLD STONE BENCH

EILEEN C. MCDONOUGH

When people learn you were raised in a cemetery, they tend to regard you in a different light. But a graveyard is just like any other type of yard; there are just more things to mow around.

Mount Moriah Cemetery in Fairview, New Jersey, served many Orthodox synagogues in the metropolitan area. Stone benches and tables encouraged the faithful to rest and reminisce when they came to pay their respects. One such bench was positioned just beyond the fence next to my playhouse, allowing me to "visit" with the cemetery's temporary and permanent guests.

One frail, older gentleman was a regular Sunday visitor whenever the weather was clear, taking two buses and walking the last half-mile. Dressed impeccably in a black suit, tie, and homburg, Mr. Wiesenthal looked far different from the way my father looked in his Sunday best. He would carry a newspaper, a bag containing an apple and some cookies, and a thermos of tea.

I would be waiting with a drink and whatever cookies my mother deemed kosher, and he and I would share our snacks and visit. With a shiny stainless steel knife, he would peel and core the apple, returning the peelings to the bag and passing slices to me through the fence. Then he would read parts of the Hebrew paper to me and to the "residents" he'd come to visit.

I looked forward to seeing him, and when two nice Sundays passed without his arrival, I began to worry.

It was summer, and I was planning a party for my favorite dolls when I realized that the old man entering my section of the cemetery was Mr. Wiesenthal. I called to him, asking where he'd been and wondering why he'd returned on a weekday. He never spoke but walked slowly around, touching each tombstone. Then he took his place on the old stone bench. I called again, realizing that his bag of goodies was not in evidence, and offered to share my doll's meager fare. The old man smiled at me and turned away as I ran into the house to find more food.

The bench was empty when I returned and I was terribly disappointed, as only a child can be. But within an hour the crew arrived to prepare a new grave site. Orthodox funerals must take place before sundown of the next day, and I shamefully enjoyed the pomp and circumstance.

The crewmen were familiar people, known to me and my family, so as they rested on the old stone bench I shared my extra bounty with them. I told them of seeing Mr. Wiesenthal, asking whether they had seen him leave. The foreman stared at me for a moment, startled. As he rose from the bench, a glint of steel caught his eye.

Mr. Wiesenthal's stainless steel pocketknife lay shiny and clean beneath the bench. It confirmed my seeing him, and I felt vindicated.

It was not until later in the day, when the cemetery's rabbi paid my parents a visit, that I learned that the funeral was for Mr. Wiesenthal. He had passed away earlier that morning.

I attended Mr. Wiesenthal's funeral from my vantage point, but I never "saw" him again.

A PHONE CALL FROM MY GRANDFATHER

LINDA J. LOVENSTEIN

I became very close to my grandfather in his later years. He was a bit eccentric and somewhat of a bigot—a cross between Jackie Gleason and Archie Bunker. He was the type who stashed $60,000 in the wheel well of his car and his opinions were always based on "fact." When I was leaving for England my wise old gramps told me that Europe was trash and that while I was young and had time, I had better see America first because that's what counted now, America! His name was Joseph Stanley Kraft.

Anyhow, my grandfather had a voice that sounded like sandpaper on petrified wood. No one could mimic the sound and no one came close, except maybe Redd Foxx. He and my parents took me to the airport when I was leaving for London. The trip was a lifelong dream—no one has ever said that I listen well to my elders as perhaps I should. They kissed me good-bye, and I was gone for a month, nineteen years old and ready to see and conquer the world.

I came home from Europe in July 1980. My grandfather was sixty-four years old. We continued our relationship, with Gramps dragging me to every ethnic restaurant in town and introducing me as his grand-daughter. I loved that man more than words can say. He was gruff, but he never fooled me for a moment—he was a big mush.

One day in August I was in the basement watching television. My father was home but I don't recall where my mother was. The phone was ringing, and I picked it up on the third ring. I heard the static of long distance and a slight ping that told me that it really was long distance—I thought it was a friend of mine calling me from London. It was about 8:00 p.m. The call immediately disconnected, and as soon as I hung up, the phone rang again. I knew that long-distance calls cannot be reconnected that fast. Upon picking up the phone again and saying,

"Hello, hello!" I heard my grandfather say, "Tell your mother that I'm fine, okay?" and I said, "Sure Grampa." Before I could ask him where he was, the phone went dead.

I then went upstairs and saw my father walking toward me with a grim expression on his face. He told me that my grandfather had passed away earlier, at 6:00 p.m. at a nearby hospital. What my brain couldn't comprehend was that I had just spoken with him, and it was two hours past 6:00 p.m. No one would be able to imitate that voice.

For the next year I kept the phone call to myself. I didn't know whether I'd somehow been aware that he was dying and had wanted one last interaction or whether I was losing my mind.

Three years after my grandfather died, I decided to do some research into our genealogy and was told by all of the relatives that my grandfather's parents were the first from their families to come to America, from Germany. I could not locate any information on relatives who had lived before his parents and became frustrated. Soon after that, I dreamed that my grandfather walked me through his parents' cemetery and pointed to the graves of his grandparents, who were never supposed to have come to America. I later went to this cemetery and walked to the older section. And right where I was led in my dream were the graves of my great-great-grandparents and their sons and daughters, whom no one in the family even knew or remembered. I believe that Gramps gave me the clue to finding them and determining when my ancestors came here (which was in 1878).

He always had to have the last word anyhow.

That's my story. It's a true one. No one can say my grandfather "died and went to heaven." I believe he kicks me in the can every once in a while to let me know he knows exactly what I'm doing.

THE VISITOR

JOAN I. JUINTA

I woke up with a start, feeling that someone was in our bedroom. There was enough light from the night-light in the hall for me to see clearly that the room was empty, but the feeling persisted. This continued to happen for many nights, I would awake in the morning with the feeling that someone was trying to tell me something. For a while I thought it was my dreams playing tricks with me, but I soon began to feel it was the spirit of a loved one. After a while I became convinced that it was my father.

After many nights of interrupted sleep, one night, frustrated, I yelled out, "If that's you, Dad, give me a sign." Feeling very foolish, I rolled over and went back to sleep. The next morning, after the family was off for the day, I went into the family room to straighten up. In the silence I heard "tick, tick, tick," and turned to see that a clock that had been broken for five years and permanently read 11:10 was now working and read *the exact* time as my wristwatch, 8:20.

That night my visitor returned and I felt the bed indent, as if someone had sat down. Although I could neither see nor hear anything, I felt no sense of fear. I was that sure my visitor was my father. At this point I expected some kind of a message or, I hoped, a visual materialization, but there was none. In a short time the feeling of this presence left. It was a long time before I fell back to sleep.

I awoke the next morning with unrelated thoughts running through my mind—don't buy a new television set, December 1, the numbers 5 and 4, love Mom. A week later two things happened: our television set broke down and a day later, December 1, 1979, while my mother was visiting us, she had a stroke. She was rushed to the hospital. We worried she would not survive the night and stayed with her until she was stable. Leaving the hospital, I took her jewelry with us—her rings, watch, and a gold locket. Returning home I opened the locket, which held pictures of my parents taken many years ago. I showed the pictures to my husband, children, and niece and then carefully closed the locket. Before going to bed I placed the jewelry on my dresser. I slept little, if at all, that night, and when I got up in the morning the locket was open and my mother's picture was gone.

We looked all over and to this day have not found her picture. My mother never recovered from her stroke and died two and a half years later, on 5-4-81. As for the television set, my mother had a brand-new color console TV that sits in our home today.

THE PROMISE

KITTY LAFOUNTAIN

It seemed as if there was an early morning fog drifting around the dining room table. It was a familiar scene. My granddad sat at the head of the table, my three uncles sat on one side of the table, and my dad and his friends sat across from them. They were playing poker and each man had a solemn look on his face. I glanced at my granddad's face. He smiled at me and then lowered his head down on his fanned-out cards. Blood slowly spread across the table. I knew he had passed away. Then I heard a woman's soft voice calling my name. It seemed so far away as she spoke, saying, "Kitty, you're sleepwalking; come back to bed." I followed the distant figure back to my room. I heard another voice saying, "It's 3:00 a.m.; I hope I get back to sleep."

I awoke the next morning when I heard the phone ringing. I heard my sister Sandra gasp and begin to cry. My uncle had informed her of our granddad's death, which had happened around three that morning. My sister's friend Marilyn had spent the night at our house and had never before witnessed a sleepwalker or heard (as she later explained) such a chilling voice speak the words, "They are all dead." My sister explained that I had run from my bedroom, entered the dining area, and slowly pointed to each chair. With my finger pointing at the head of the table, I had spoken those chilling words.

My granddad had had lung cancer and had been hospitalized for a few months. Prior to his death he had spoken to me about his death and his desire that I view his passing as a joy and comfort, as he would be with his heavenly Father. He asked me not to cry but to be happy and to wear white at his funeral. He had also given me his special witch hazel cologne, and he had said he would always be with me. I had placed the cologne in our linen closet for safekeeping behind the sheets on the seldom-used top shelf.

After my sister and her friend Marilyn left our house that morning, I sat on our living room sofa trying to remember Granddad's last words to me. When I started to cry our family poodle started howling and wouldn't stop. I then smelled the familiar scent of witch hazel. I ran to the linen closet and when I opened it, I discovered that the bottle had fallen and its contents had spilled on the floor. Its aroma filled the house and brought me instant peace. I knew Granddad was there, but unfortunately so did the dog; he continued to howl. I silently vowed once again to Granddad that I would not cry but rejoice at his peace. The dog stopped his howling shortly thereafter.

And yes, I kept my promise to Granddad, but that's another story.

A GENTLE GOOD-BYE

MARTHA ROCK

The flu epidemic was raging through the rural Pennsylvania area where my mother lived. Her father was gravely ill. Her mother had the flu also, but not as severely. It was necessary to bring in a nurse to care for them. My mother was sixteen—the oldest daughter and very close to her father. She did all that she could to help with his care.

It was a stormy night, with loud crashes of thunder and lightning flashing about. Her father had developed a high fever and was shaking with chills. The nurse asked for another blanket, so my mother went to the attic where they were stored. There was another deafening crack of thunder and a sudden silence. Then there was the firm but gentle pressure of a hand on her shoulder. Terrified, she turned and ran back to the sick room. The nurse looked at her empty hands and said gently, "He has no need of a blanket now. Your father passed away just a few minutes ago."

LOST LOVE

BARBARA ERCOLE

When most people think of a ghost, they think of things that go bump in the night, frightening and horrifying. The ghost that came to me was most welcome.

Twenty years ago I met and planned to marry the man who is presently my husband. We were into our courtship and had set a wedding date when I met another young man.

We happened to become good friends and saw each other quite often because we shared the same employer. He told me he felt drawn to me, and I told him I felt the same way, but that perhaps the attraction was there because of my premarital jitters. As I look back, I know that I was wrong. He had such a gentle way about him—he will always be remembered.

My husband and I were soon married, and I have no regrets—two wonderful children, a nice home, and a good man. A few years passed, but deep in my heart I secretly wondered about John—my secret thoughts, and only mine.

One evening I was extremely tired and went to sleep early—I call it the sleep of the dead. I dreamed that John had died, but yet he was somehow living and had come to visit me as I lay in bed asleep. He didn't frighten me, and the dream itself was beautiful and very vivid. He kissed my cheek very gently, told me he loved me, and said he was leaving now. I watched him go, all the while reaching out to him, still feeling the warmth of the gentle kiss, it being imparted with such love and tenderness.

I awoke abruptly and looked around. Certainly this must have been real, but there was no one there. But my cheek felt warm—as I reached up to feel it, I wiped what seemed like a bit of moisture where I had felt the tender kiss. The nightstand clock read 1:30 a.m. I floated back into sleep again.

The next day, while reading the local newspaper, I spotted an article with a picture of a car accident. John had died at the hospital, according to the newspaper report, at 1:20 a.m.

I supposed John's visit was just a dream, but what a pleasant one. A dream, maybe, but also a fond good-bye. To John, my welcome ghost, my friend, a lost love—till we meet again . . .

COMING BACK FOR MAMMIE

STEVEN G. O'CONNELL

On June 19, 1970, my grandfather, Joseph Kennington, passed away. He was the only one of a family of seven children to leave his beloved homeland of Ireland and travel far across the Atlantic to the United States. He managed well, as did many in this "land of opportunity."

Because his mother was 103 years old upon his death, it was decided by those still in Ireland not to tell my great-grandmother that her youngest son had died. They were afraid that the stress on her heart would kill her. For one full year she had no knowledge of her son's death.

Letters were written to my grandmother, Kathleen, by my great-grandmother, Mammie (as they called her in Ireland), asking, "How's

Joe?" Kathleen, who was torn up inside, felt a terrible guilt at keeping her husband's death a secret. But because of the family's request, she wrote back, "He's doing well. He's in good hands." There weren't any phones in the Irish home, which made it easier to keep Joe's passing a secret.

One year later, almost to the day my grandfather died, Mammie became deathly ill. She came down with the chills early in the day and that evening developed a fever of 103 degrees. She slept most of the day, everyone taking turns sitting bedside in an hour-by-hour rotation, wiping her moist brow with a damp cloth while she mumbled in both Gaelic (the ancient Irish language) and English, "Is that you, Joe?"

It was difficult tending to her that evening. Several times those who sat at her bedside watched as her breathing became very shallow; her skin was pallid and deathly white. Those around her knew she might not make it through the night. She continually mumbled, sometimes forcing her withered body up into a sitting position and shouting, "Where's Joe?" and "Is that you, Joe? Come here by the light and let me see your face."

The next morning the fever had passed and those at her bedside watched as Mammie slowly showed signs of recovery. The blood returned to her face, her cheeks becoming rosy red. She told them that she had had a strange dream late last night that Joe, wearing a lovely new blue suit, had come to visit her. His cheeks were rosy. He smiled at her and sat beside her, holding her hand. She also went on to say that she had looked down at his feet to see that he had no shoes on. When she questioned his lack of shoes, something strange occurred.

"Joe," she asked, "you look so handsome in your blue suit, but where are your shoes?" She went on to say that he stiffened up and his face became as white as milk. Then he said to her, "Mum, I'm dead. I'm dead."

Those who stood around her as she told the tale were in awe. They knew there was no way she could have any idea that Joe was already dead. And how could she have known he was buried in a blue suit? That night, Mammie again took ill, this time for the worse. At about 3:05 a.m., she awoke my great-aunt, Peggy (whose turn it was in the rotation), by loudly saying, "It's Joe, he's come back to see me. He looks so lovely, so grand in his nice blue suit. He's come back for me."

That was what Great-aunt Peggy told everyone the next morning. My great-grandmother had passed away. She died with no knowledge of her son's passing one year earlier, but somehow, believe it or not, he had managed to navigate the netherworld in a last attempt to let her know he hadn't forgotten her.

A mother's love for her son is great, but a son's love for his mother is not rivaled.

GRANDMOTHER'S WARNING

JANE MEGGITT

Early one Sunday morning in 1983, my grandmother, seven years dead, appeared at my bedside. The digital clock next to the bed read 6:02 a.m. Grandma stood right beside the bed, and she was telling me to call an ambulance for my aunt (her daughter). She explained that my aunt was very sick and must get to a hospital.

When I opened my eyes, the clock read 6:03 a.m. Had it been a dream? If so, it was unlike any dream I have had before or since, and the only dream I ever had in which the unities of time and space were observed.

Puzzled and a bit frightened, I woke up my sleeping husband and told him what had happened. He assured me that it must have been a dream and advised me to go back to sleep.

A few days later, I spoke with my mother who told me that my aunt, who lives in Florida, was back home after being rushed to the hospital Sunday morning. She had apparently suffered a severe asthma attack and was unable at first to alert her husband, who was sleeping in another room. He finally heard her and summoned an ambulance.

Was my grandmother trying to pierce the veil between this world and the next to save a loved one? I'm not certain, but I did tell my aunt that she had better be on her best behavior, because her mother was still watching over her.

A HOMEOWNER'S RETURN

MARTIN VIDANA

In 1974 my wife and I purchased a beautiful home from an elderly couple. The husband had had a heart attack and was in poor health, so they were moving to be closer to relatives. We became good friends with them during the escrow period and were sad to see them leave. The husband was particularly sad to leave this home, as he loved it very much and had taken excellent care of it.

Some years later, early one morning at about 12:30 a.m., I arrived home from working a graveyard shift. I heard our dog crying and whimpering strangely. I was in the kitchen at the time and walked over to the sliding glass doors to see what was wrong with him. These glass doors led out to the patio, which had a concrete floor and gravel surrounding it. The gravel made crunching sounds when we walked on it.

I turned on the patio light and was just about to unlatch the door to go outside when suddenly I saw a figure moving from my right, above the gravel. As I watched it, it continued to move to my left and seemed to glide right through the patio furniture and wooden slats that bordered the patio. I was able to see the objects on the patio right through the figure. The figure moved to my left and out of sight.

My heart was racing, as the figure had not made any noise while in motion, not even as it glided over the gravel. At this point my mind was not fully comprehending; I would not believe what I had seen take place.

I once again became concerned about our dog, as he had suddenly become silent, and I wanted to go check on him. I looked in the closet for something that I could use to defend myself, if necessary. I was trying to convince myself that it wasn't a ghost but perhaps an intruder.

My wife, upon hearing my rummaging about, came downstairs to see what was going on. She was immediately alarmed when she saw me and thought I was having a heart attack or that I was very ill. I had turned white and was visibly shaken.

Her first reaction, when I told her what I had seen, was skepticism. But she also knew that I didn't believe in ghosts; just seeing the state I was in made her believe that I had seen *something*. We tried to come up with possible explanations for what I had seen. I knew that whatever it was could not be fully explained, but I was afraid to use the actual word "ghost."

A few days later, while reading our local newspaper, I happened to read the obituary of a former resident who had died out of state. I suddenly realized that it was the old owner of our home, the husband. I also realized that the date of his death coincided with the day when, in the early morning hours, I had seen the figure.

MY UNCLE KEN

DONALD S. CAMPBELL

Twice my uncle Ken has had eerie experiences at precisely the same moment, in the early morning hours.

The first time, he was serving aboard a U.S. Navy destroyer in the Pacific during World War II. My mother, who lived in Boston at that time, awoke at 12:15 a.m. when she heard someone calling her name. The voice sounded like her brother's. For no other reason than that, she wrote down the time and date.

In the days following, letters came to the house saying that Uncle Ken was fine. The family soon discovered, however, that Uncle Ken had been knocked unconscious during heavy bombardment in a Japanese attack at the precise time that my mother had heard his voice.

Years later, Uncle Ken was awakened suddenly during a hurricane. Although he does not know why, he left his house, barefoot and clad in his pajamas, and walked to the road a few feet from his driveway. He was met on the road by a black car and the rear window rolled down to reveal his father who, at the time, lived in northern Maine. His father said to him, "I just wanted to say good-bye."

The next thing my uncle remembers is waking up in bed that morning to his wife's complaints about muddy footprints tracked through the house.

Later that day the local police arrived with bad news. They explained that they had not been able to contact him sooner because the hurricane had blown out all the phone lines.

But, of course, Uncle Ken already knew that his father had passed away the night before—at exactly 12:15 a.m.

GHOST IN A GOLF CAP

JOHN S. TRANT, SR.

I was working as a pinspotter in a bowling alley at Hampton Beach, New Hampshire, that summer of 1946. Damp, raw weather had driven most vacationers inside. All lanes were busy and the place was bustling, with the constant crashing of bowling pins and the clamor of exuberant bowlers.

Suddenly I sensed someone staring at me. Glancing up from the pit I saw my grandfather standing at the end of the lane. I felt a twinge of fear for it had been three months since I had run away from home.

For a moment I thought it must be someone else. Grandfather did not like the beach. But there was no mistaking his piercing, agate-blue eyes, his luxuriant iron-gray mustache, and his powerful frame—slightly stooped from years of bending over the forge swinging a five-pound sledgehammer.

He raised his hand and waved to me. Even from the span of seventy-five feet I could see the blue mark between his thumb and forefinger. It was the ship's anchor and chain he had had tattooed on his right hand after joining the Swedish Royal Navy.

He tugged his golf cap, a characteristic gesture, and then vanished.

Haunted by the prospect of being dragged home by the authorities, I got little sleep that night. The mysterious appearance of my grandfather was even more upsetting, for I was certain no one at home had known my whereabouts.

Striking out the following morning, I hitchhiked the forty-odd miles home. As I neared our house I felt a sudden compulsion to visit the cemetery, which lay only a few blocks from my house.

Approaching our family plot I saw a fresh grave banked high with flowers. I picked up a floral spray and the gold lettering on the gray silk ribbon read "Grandfather."

Entering my home I asked, "When did Pa die?"

"We buried him yesterday," my mother replied.

My grandparents had raised me until I was five. Over the years our family would inevitably end up back in their home when my father, who was in the military, was posted in various parts of the world. During my formative years my grandfather served as my male role model, and we were close. As I grew older we drifted apart. I was a typical smart-aleck teenager.

I can only assume that the bond forged in my childhood was powerful enough to enable my grandfather to touch me from beyond the grave. His fleeting appearance was more than a farewell. It propelled me home to assume my responsibilities as "the man of the house."

GENERATIONS

LINDA ANGELL

My mother opened her eyes and froze in absolute terror, too frightened to move or even call for her parents, who were in the next room. Three people surrounded her bed. They stood there silently peering at her. Looking frantically around, she realized there was no way they could have gotten in there without her hearing them, but they were definitely there.

Discovering that one of them was her grandmother did nothing but add to the horror. Her grandmother, a stern-faced old woman who had always ruled her family with an iron hand, was dead. She had died the year before.

The three began to talk to her. They said that they had come to take her uncle Irvin away from his pain and suffering. A sudden surge of adrenaline allowed her to leap from the bed and race to her parents' room. Her father was quick to comfort his eldest child, telling her that it was just a bad dream.

But morning brought a phone call saying that Irvin had died from cancer during the night.

Several years passed and my mother, now a young wife, was forced to watch her own father die the same long, excruciating death that his brother Irvin had. My father awoke one night and found her sitting straight up in bed, very distraught. He asked her what was wrong, and she said, "It's Daddy. You talk to him. He can't hear me." My father did not see anyone there, but he reached out to comfort my mother. Just then the phone rang. It was the hospital calling to tell them that my grandfather had passed on a few moments before.

My husband and I adopted two children before I gave birth to our youngest son. Whenever we visited my parents, all five of us would sleep in the same downstairs bedroom. Our children, like all children, often objected to staying in bed because they heard "sounds" or saw "things." We, like all parents, assured them that nothing was there—

until the afternoon my mother, my grandmother, and I were cleaning out the closet in the library.

Coming across some old pictures, my mother suddenly turned pale. "That is the same man I saw in my room when Uncle Irvin died," she whispered. We all sat staring at the picture when my youngest child came in, crawled up on my lap, and, in his lisping baby voice, exclaimed, "Dat's da tall man who wooks at me when I got to go to bed here! He pways ball wif a wittle boy."

This time it was my grandmother who was visibly shaken. The man was my mother's great-grandfather, whom she had never met! The room we slept in had been the family parlor in his time.

SISTERS

DENISE LENAHAN MANNING

On March 11, 1982, my sister—Karen Lee Lenahan, then nineteen years old—died in a violent car accident.

When our family was selecting Karen's burial clothing, I insisted that one of our favorite pierced earrings be placed in one of her earlobes. You see, Karen had borrowed this favorite pair of earrings from me a few months earlier, only to lose one of the earrings.

A few weeks after her death, I was in church, attending a Good Friday service. During the service, I felt especially close to my sister and was spiritually moved. That evening as I slept, Karen came to me in a dream. She looked so beautiful, surrounded by a glowing white light. Karen told me about the car accident and said that she was now at peace and with the Lord. Karen also asked me to tell our family about her visit and to relate her messages. Karen's final words were that she loved me, to tell our family that she loved them, too, and that she would see them again someday.

The next morning I felt relieved and at peace. While my husband, Dave, and I made our bed, I told him of my dream. As we were finishing making the bed, Dave bent down. There on the carpet was the mate to the earring that Karen had been buried with.

Finding the mate to the lost earring was a confirmation that Karen had indeed come to visit, and that, someday, I will see my sister again.

HE GOT THERE FIRST

CHERYL M. CONDON

Do you remember when John Lennon died? I do, vividly.

It was the first year of my marriage and I was just twenty-three. I watched television most of the night, as I wanted to know more about this upsetting tragedy. It was the first time I had an understanding of the loss people feel when a celebrity dies. Even though you've never met that person, he or she is a part of you. I thought back to when John F. Kennedy died. I remember seeing the pain people felt. I remember little John Kennedy, Jr., waving a flag during his father's funeral procession.

How could someone just take another person's life without regard for it? I waited for the ten o'clock news to learn more about Lennon's death. I felt angry and empty. Then, just before the news ended, another story came on the screen. The driver of a car racing down a street near my home had lost control and hit a truck, causing the car to roll and crash into a house. How awful! Luckily, only the driver of the out-of-control car was killed. The accident took place just two blocks from where I lived. Already angry, I was upset that the driver had almost taken innocent victims with him when he died.

The next evening my husband and I were getting ready to go over to a friend's house. I remember reaching for my coat, which was on the chair. A cool breeze ran through me. That must be what it feels like when a *ghost* runs through you—this was my exact thought. Then I laughed at myself for having such an overactive imagination. The front door was open, and I was sure it was just a well-directed breeze.

I spoke about death and grieving with my husband all the way to our friend's house. I talked about all the people I had lost and how I missed them. We passed a funeral parlor and I even thought of Yoko Ono sitting in one. She must be very sad, I thought.

When we reached our friend's house I called my mother, though I have no idea why. I don't usually call Mom from other people's houses.

"I am so glad you called," was her reply. "I have been trying to get ahold of you. What was your high school sweetheart's full name?"

I thought that was a pretty strange question for my mom to ask, but I answered it anyway.

"Honey, he was killed in an awful car accident. His car hit a truck and a house. It was right by your house!" cried Mom.

"Oh my God! I saw that on the ten o'clock news last night!" I said. "That's impossible!"

"Why, Mom?"

"Because it happened at 2:00 a.m. . . . . this morning!"

Mom and I tried to sort out the details, and we could never make sense of it. My old friend died the day after John Lennon. Maybe the paper was wrong, the news was wrong, or I was just mixed up. Now the entire event feels like a dream, but it really happened.

My old friend's message, however, was clear. When we were dating, we disagreed on supernatural things. He was an atheist. I am sure at one point we promised that whoever found the answers first would tell the other one.

I no longer wonder whether there is life after death. I know there is, thanks to my ghost.